Machine Learning with Python:

A Step-By-Step Guide in Learning

from Scratch Machine Learning and

Deep Learning with Python, a

Practical Learning with Scikit-Learn

and Tensor Flow with Examples

Mark J. Branson

Table of Contents

Introduction

Congratulations on the purchase of the book *Machine Learning with Python* and thank you for doing so.

The following chapters will discuss in detail about machine learning and its implementation in python using tensor flow and scikit learn. Machine learning has been in a boom in the tech industry from a couple of years. There are multiple reasons and instances that made the machine learning a developer's favorite. It can be used for facial recognition and textual interpretation systems and in a lot of software and applications.

This book is a comprehensive outing of knowledge that will help you understand more about machine learning and neural networks in detail with sci-kit learn and Tensor Flow.

Since the invention of the computer, the realization of Artificial Intelligence (AI) has become the goal of generations of scientists and technologists. In the process of seeking solutions, people have encountered many difficult problems at the same time, many attempts have been made to overcome these difficulties.

With the development of the Times, a large number of network applications have appeared in people's lives. The emergence of various intelligent devices has made the collection of data a reality. At the same time, the computing power of computers has been greatly improved how to extract valuable information from large amounts of data has become a very important topic, machine learning is such a tool to extract useful information from unordered data.

Machine learning can extract useful information from unordered data, so what is machine learning? Take spam detection as an example, spam detection is to be able to make a judgment on the mail, determine whether it is spam or normal mail.

In the early days of artificial intelligence, people tried to solve many problems by handwriting rules. For example, in spam detection, a message is likely to be spam when some pre-specified words that might be spam appear in the message, and it is also likely to be spam when a link appears in the message. To some extent, these rules play a role in the detection of spam, but with more rules, such a detection system becomes more and more complex. At this time, people found that the fundamental way to solve this problem is how to automatically learn from some of the characteristics of the data between them, and with the continuous learning of the data, improve the performance of garbage detection.

Machine learning is to learn and extract useful information from data to improve the performance of the machine. So, an important part of a specific machine learning problem is the collection of data that we call training data. The basic job of machine learning is to learn rules from the data and use them to predict new data.

The next chapters, in brief, will discuss various, algorithms and concepts of machine learning in detail. Let us dive into the programmatically implementation of machine learning.

There are plenty of books on this subject on the market, thanks again for choosing this one! Every effort was made to ensure it is full of as much useful information as possible, please enjoy!

Chapter 1: Introduction to machine learning

This chapter will help you give a detailed explanation of machine learning in layman's terms. We will start with a little bit of history and will dive into the categories explanation that will help you understand things in the real-world view.

History of machine learning

Humans have always tried to make machines intelligent that is by using Artificial Intelligence. From the 1950s, the development of artificial intelligence experienced the "inference period." By giving the machine logical reasoning ability to make the machine intelligent, the AI program at that time can prove some famous mathematical theorems, but because the machine lacks knowledge, it is far from real Intelligence. Therefore, in the 1970s, the development of artificial intelligence entered the "knowledge period," which summed up human knowledge and taught it to machines to make machines acquire intelligence.

During this period, a large number of expert systems came out and achieved a lot of results in many fields. However, due to the huge amount of human knowledge, there was a "knowledge bottleneck in knowledge engineering." Whether it is the "inference period" or the "knowledge period," the machine operates according to the rules set by humans and the summarized knowledge, and can never surpass its creators. Secondly, the labor cost is too high.

Therefore, some scholars have thought that if the machine can self-learn problems, it will not be solved. The Machine Learning method came into being, and artificial intelligence entered the machine learning period. Machine learning is said to have many stages during its reign. In the years of 1980s neural networks have been in a significant rise.

And in the nineties, we saw a very much wave for statistically learning methods. In the 21st century, deep neural networks were proposed. Connectionism has never been seen, with the increasing amount of data and computing power. Many AI applications based on Deep Learning have matured. Therefore, artificial intelligence is the pursuit of goals, machine learning is the means to achieve, and deep learning is one of them.

What is Machine learning?

Machine learning is a branch of computer science in which a special power is given to computers that are to improve them by writing their own code and consuming data. Technically, machine learning gets better with training. Machine learning is also divided into different sub-branches like deep learning and reinforcement learning.

Machine learning steps

Usually learn a good function, divided into the following three steps:

1) Choose a suitable model, which usually depends on the actual problem, for different problems and tasks need to choose the appropriate model, the model is a collection of functions.

2) To determine the quality of a function, this needs to determine a metric, which is what we usually call Loss Function (Loss Function), the determination of the loss function also needs to be based on specific issues, such as regression problems generally use Euclidean distance, classification The problem generally uses a cross-entropy cost function.

3) Find out the "best" function, how to find the "best" one from the fastest of many functions, this step is the biggest difficulty, it is often not an easy task to achieve fast and accurate. Commonly used methods are gradient descent algorithm, least-squares method, and other tricks.

After learning the "best" function, you need to test it on a new sample. It is a "good" function only if it performs well on the new sample.

Machine Learning Roadmap

Machine learning is a huge family system involving many algorithms, tasks and learning theories. The following figure is a learning road map for machine learning.

1. According to the task type

Machine learning can also be further divided based on the type of task. It can be divided based on regression and classification methods. Apart from this we also have a structured learning method which is quite famous with data scientists. When we use this category, we always get a numerical value as the output. When we go further, we will understand that classification and multi-classification both exist. The common two-category problem is spam filtering. Common multi-classification problems are automatically classified by documents. It is to be a noted fact that when using a structured model we no longer get fixed value as output due to various reasons.

2) From the perspective of methods

We can also further differentiate them based on their acceptance with linearity as linear and not obeying as non-linear models. linear models are the basis of nonlinear models, many nonlinear models are based on linear models Come. Nonlinear models are also distinguished as models that are old and scientifically sound such as SVM, KNN, decision trees, etc., and deep learning models.

3) According to the learning theory

The machine learning model can be divided into supervised learning, semi-supervised learning, unsupervised learning, migration learning, and reinforcement learning. When the training sample is tagged, there is supervised learning; the training sample part has a label, and some of the training samples are semi-supervised learning; when the training samples are all unlabeled, it is unsupervised learning.

Migration learning is a basic learning model because it just uses already trained parameters to be incorporated into a new model to improve its performance.

Reinforcement learning is a learning optimal strategy that allows an agent to make an action in a particular environment based on the current state, thereby achieving the maximum reward. The biggest difference between intensive and supervised learning is that each decision is not right or wrong, but rather the most cumulative reward.

A detailed explanation of machine learning and how it works

Machine Learning = Representation + Evaluation + Optimization

Representation refers to how the output is derived from the input. Evaluation refers to estimating the distribution of the output or input. Optimization is used to approximate the distribution.

Machine learning is to fit the true distribution to get an unknown distribution. For solving two types of problems, one is the classification problem classification, the input is given, the output is independent and the classification is determined. The other is the regression problem regression. For the given input, the trained model can predict the output value, and the output value is continuously distributed.

Learning Classification

Supervised learning:

Training examples with a label (output known), such as handwriting recognition, aim to infer the unknown based on the known mapping relationship, and can quickly give a new point label with a small amount of calculation.

Unsupervised learning:

Training without label example does not produce input to output mapping but also has an objective function, which is also optimized for the objective function.

Semi-supervised learning: The Combination of the Two
Transduction:
The specific training set observed to predict a particular fixed test set, the key is reasoning, not the inductive model, which is derived from the contradictory speculation of some test sets (TSVM), which is used to obtain better approximations, and The test set can be

arbitrarily distributed, while the semi-supervised is related to the training set. The benefit is that fewer labeled points are needed to predict the classification, and all points can be considered, marking which unlabeled points belong to which cluster they belong to. The disadvantage is that the prediction model will not be built. If there is a new point insertion, then all the points need to be traversed again. There is a piece of famous scientific evidence that says how much complexity the model entails its regularization increases.

Enhanced Learning:

Related to behavioral psychology, the environment is the Markov Decision Process (MDP), which is related to dynamic programming techniques. It is not necessary to know the specific MDP because it needs to solve very large MDP. The difference is that there is no correct input-output pair, and the behavior of finding the wrong label is not corrected. The focus is on continuous performance, finding a balance between unexplored and developed areas. For example, in a gambling machine, to get the maximum output value, and not mind what the combination is, the gambler should find the arm that gets the most reward as soon as possible. There are many combinations, only the best combination.

Multitasking:

Learn multiple related problems in parallel, multiple labels? For example, mail filtering, individual spam is different, but it must be the same, for example, you can make all the weight values smaller. It is used to predict the output without a given input. Through the previous training experience, a certain output (example) is trained, even if it is not found in the training set, but it can be inferred. Inductive bias makes some assumptions (premise) on the target concept. A few important concepts in machine learning.

Generalization:

This is to separate the test set from the training set. The distribution obtained by overfitting is close to the training set, but the test set is not approached. At this time, the objective function will take care of each point, resulting in the formation of the proposed the function fluctuates greatly, and the derivative of each place is large, so that although all the points are included, the function change is very complicated, and only the coefficient is enough to ensure that the derivative value is large. Cross-validation can help avoid overfitting (that is, using validation set validation). The general way to avoid is to add a regularization term. The regularization term is generally a monotonically increasing function of the complexity of the model.

Occam razor principle:

This principle is called "if it is not necessary, do not increase the entity," the simpler the better.

Inductive Bias:

The search path is the core problem of the machine learning algorithm. The optimal path is found. With the gradient descent method, the search range is defined as the inductive bias. With it, when the weight is changed step by step. At the time, it is also approaching the equilibrium point step by step.

Features:

In fact, the features are composed little by little. Small features combine to form large features. The upper layer looks at the pixel level, and the next layer is called the upper layer of the basic layer. Is another representation of the input, there can be no loss of information.

Python and machine learning:

This book basically uses python due to its huge number of models and good correlation with the machine learning applications primarily because of its natural advantages, and because, in machine learning algorithms, a great deal of Linear Algebra is involved The NumPy function library is available in Python specifically for dealing with a variety of LINEAR algebra problems.

Python has many advantages, such as 1 the Python community has a large library that almost solves most problems; 2 Python is known as the Glue Language and can be mixed compiled using libraries such as C / C + + Java; 3 the Python Syntax is simple and easy to operate.

For Python, however, the only drawback is performance. Python programs don' t run as efficiently as Java or C. However, Python provides methods to invoke both languages, so it's computationally demanding it can be implemented in either C or Java, taking advantage of both Python's ease of use and C's efficiency. Python language performance is not the focus of this book, so there will be no mention of Python performance in this book.

This chapter ends in this way. Hope this chapter gave you a brief overview of machine learning concepts and some important terminology that you can use to improve your efficiency in this subject. In the next chapter, we will try to understand the machine learning project structure in detail.

Chapter 2: Machine learning project structure

In the previous chapter, we have learned in detail about machine learning and its importance along with a lot of categories and classifications that might have given you a surface level knowledge about this expertise. But to be a successful data scientist you need to master different concepts along with a classical structural format that machine learning enthusiasts use to solve a real-world problem. This chapter in detail will help you achieve this with an example and detailed explanation.

We will divide the process into eight basic steps so that it would be easy for you to follow the procedure. Here are the eight-point criteria.

1) See the problem in a universal view
2) Obtain the data that is needed
3) Research the data using visualization methods to understand what it offers

4) Make the data perfect so that it can be used in algorithms

5) Create a model and give the data for training

6) Make your model perfect and feasible

7) Give a perfect solution to the real-world problem

8) Now maintain and use the system and keep an eye on it every second.

Before going into a dive into the machine learning world remember that data is easy to obtain in this technological world. The world is moving rapidly and people are very judgmental about their privacy. So never try to use data that you have obtained illegally. Also, there are many software's that offer artificial datasets for testing and training purposes. While these datasets can be used to master the techniques of machine learning and data analysis when creating a model for real-world problems these can give very bad results as they are far away from reality.

Where can we obtain data that is useful?

Several data scientists have tried to solve this problem by sharing data that is feasible and can solve problems. Websites like Kaggle can be used to obtain datasets that can be trained and experimented. Special datasets for example like IMDB dataset, Wikipedia Dataset, Quora and Reddit datasets can be obtained from their respective websites. While most of the companies give datasets for free some may charge a nominal price various reason.

In the next sections, we will discuss the eight-step criteria in detail with examples. Follow on!

1) See the problem in a universal view

In this example, the problem we are going to solve is about

We will divide this into three basic strategies

    a) Understand the problem

    b) Decide a performance measure

    c) Crosscheck

2) Obtain the data that is needed

    a) Install python

b) Install modules

c) Download the data

d) Create a test set

3) **Research the data using visualization methods to understand what it offers**

    a) Visualizing review data

    b) Looking for correlations

    c) Try various attribute combinations

4) **Make the data perfect so that it can be used in algorithms**

    a) Data cleaning

    b) Data preprocessing

    c) Custom transformers

    d) Future scaling

    e) Transformation pipelines

5) **Create a model and give the data for training**

    a) Training and evaluating on the training set

    b) Using cross-validation

6) Make your model perfect and feasible

    a) Grid search

    b) Randomized search

    c) Ensemble learning

    d) Analyze models and errors

    e) Evaluate

7) Give a perfect solution to the real-world problem

8) Now maintain and use the system and keep an eye on it every second.

We will now install python and necessary modules along with Tensor Flow in this section. Follow with a computer to understand the process.

The Python Program in this book was developed under the Python version 2.7.9, and it is recommended that you install Python 2.8 or above as of this writing.

On the Windows platform, after downloading the installation package, follow the instructions in the next step to complete the installation. When the installation is complete, open the console with Win + R and enter the following command:

c:\users\srujan>python

Start Python, and if you have it installed correctly, you can see the ver ion number for Python, among other things:

python 2.7.9

Install scikit learn and numpy:

Understand the fact that to make good machine learning applications numpy is one of the basic modules that need to be install.

Install it using the following command

pip install numpy

To install numpy, users on the Windows platform can

select the appropriate installation package via https: sourceforge.net/projects/numpy/files/numpy.

a) Data types available in python:

Python's basic data types include integers, floating-point types, booleans, strings, and more:

c = 1
# this is an integer

b = 0.3
# this is a float

c = " Debuda"

this is a stranger

b) Data structures available in python:

Data structures are important for the machine learning mechanism because they make most of the complex code.

a) list

```python
# This is a list in python
c = [3,4,32,11]
```

b) set

```python
# This is a set in python
d = set (c)
```

c) Tuple

```python
# This is a tuple in python
c = {3,7,5,1}
```

d) Dictionary

```python
# This is a dictionary in python
e = {}
e[1] = 7
e[2] = 9
```

The elements stored in the collection are distinct elements, and in the dictionary, they are stored as key: value.

c) Functions in the python

The Python function uses def to define the function, as in the symbolic function sign:

```
def number(y)
If input>3:
return x
else
input <3 : return y
else :
return null
```

Call it directly by:

```
print number(7)
```

d) Classes in python

Once the class is defined, declare and initialize it:

```
class Read:

def _init_

def print
```

e) Numpy

Whenever we hear the word scientific calculations word in python numpy will reverberate from the other side. it is easy to implement the matrix-related operations in Python.

1) Numpy Array

An array in numpy is a collection of data of the same type that can be generated by the array function in numpy:

```
import numpy as np
```

In numpy, there are other ways to create arrays:

```
b= np.array([1,7,9])
print type(b)
```

```
print b
```

Array elements in numpy can be accessed using subscript:

```
import numpy as np

d = np.zeros(({4,4])
print d
```

For Arrays, there is usually addition, subtraction, and multiplication:

Code is here:

```
print np.add(a,b)
# This is addition

print np.sub(a,b)
# This is substraction

print np.mul(a,b)
```

This is multiplcation

print np.div(a,b)
This is division

Note that in multiplication, a * B represents the multiplication of the corresponding elements, and the DOT function should be used if the Matrix Product is implemented.

f) Matrix mat

Similar to arrays, there is a representation that translates directly into a matrix:

In this way, you can use a variety of Matrix calculations, such as transpose, inverse, Matrix product, and so on:

Code is here:
```
d = np.mat(([3,4],[11,12]))
print d

print d.T
```

This will give transpose of the matrix

print d.I
This will give inverse of the matrix

Installation of Tensor flow:

For the installation of TensorFlow, the Windows platform was not supported while the book was being completed, so my experiment was done in an Ubuntu Environment. For the Ubuntu Environment, you can install the CPU version directly:

Sudo pip install-upgrade { insert tensorflow official download address here according to your time. Just do quick Google research to know the download url}

Tensorflow operations

In TensorFlow, a computational task is represented by a graph. The nodes in the graph are called operations. Each operation has 0 or more tensors, and these tensors are evaluated to produce 0 or more tensors. In TensorFlow, the operation is described as a graph, which must be started in the session in order to compute. The basic operation for TensorFlow is shown in the following sections.

Basic operations of the Tensor flow

First, to be able to use TensorFlow, we need to import TensorFlow:

```
import tensorflow as tf
```

Now we can use the basic features of TensorFlow.

```
y = tf.constant(20)
```

Definition of constants

This defines a constant x with a value of 10.

Definition of variables

In TensorFlow, variables are defined with Variable and must be initialized

In this way, we define a 33 full 1 Matrix X and a 33 full 0 Matrix Y. When the variable is defined, you must also use the following action:

In this way, the variable can be used.

a) Placeholder

We've shown that variables need to be initialized when they are defined, but if there are variables that we don't know their values at first, we can't initialize them, so we use placeholders to indicate:

This specifies the type and size of the variable.

a) Graph

In TensorFlow, to implement specific operations, such as the addition of two variables, we cannot directly define two variables and add two numbers, output results. In TensorFlow, where each variable is a tensor object and the operations between the objects are called operations (op), TensorFlow does not perform operations one by one but puts all operations into a graph Each node in the diagram is an operation. Then the entire graph calculation is given to a TensorFlow Session, which can run the entire calculation, such as calculating the addition of two variables:

Which sess. Run () is the execution of the operation. Note that the variable initialization operation is performed before the operation. The Session needs to be created first and then released after use. If you use placeholders, you need to use the feed to assign a value to the placeholder.

This is it. We now have a complete overview of machine learning project structure and also a little bit about TensorFlow, python basics and scikit learn which we deal with while implementing in the further chapters. In the next chapter, we deal with some functions which can be used to fit the model to data. Follow up!

Chapter 3: Fitting a Model to Data

In machine learning, we have always hoped to learn a function with strong generalization. Only a model with strong generalization ability can be applied to the whole sample space well so that it can perform well at new sample points. However, the training set is usually only a small part of the entire sample space. When training the machine learning model, if you pay little attention to it, you may consider the characteristics of the training set as the commonality of the whole sample. The problem of overfitting, how to avoid overfitting, is the most stumbling block to be solved when training machine learning models.

Starting from the root of the problem, there are two ways to solve the overfitting.

Enables the training set to describe the entire sample space as comprehensively as possible. Therefore, there are two solutions to the problem.

1) Reduce the feature dimension, reduce the feature dimension, and reduce the size of the sample space. The description of the sample space by the existing data set is also improved.

2) Increase the number of training samples, trying to directly improve the ability to describe the sample space.

3) Add a regularization item.

The labor cost of the first method is usually very large, so in practice, we usually use the second method to improve the generalization ability of the model.

Note: Regularization is also referred to as regularization in some documents, and regularized descriptions are used in this article.

Regularize

First of all, when looking for the optimal parameters of the model, we usually use the gradient descent algorithm for the loss function.

Through the formula, we will step by step to the lowest point of the loss function (regardless of the local minimum and saddle point), and the sum at this time is the optimal parameter we are looking for. For the regression problem, we can also use the least-squares method to obtain an analytical solution.

It can be seen that our current loss function only considers minimizing the training error, and hopes that the optimal function found can fit the training data as much as possible. But as we know, the training set can't represent the whole sample space, so the training error can't represent the test error. The training error is only an empirical risk. We can't rely too much on this value. When our function fits the training set particularly well and the training error is particularly small, we go into an extreme – overfitting.

To solve this problem, the researchers proposed a regularize method. By attaching some rules, i.e. constraints, to the model parameters, the model is prevented from over-fitting the training data.

At this point, the optimized objective function is as follows.

Among them, the first term corresponds to the error of the model represents various other functions that can be changed. To make things better in the minimalization we need minimum training error and the minimum regularization term, so we need to make a trade-off between the two.

What kind of expression should I choose as a regularization item?

The regularization term is generally a monotonically increasing function of the complexity of the model. This definitely says that the regularization vector is one of the basic entities of machine learning diaspora.

Regularization conforms to the principle of Occam's razor. The Occam razor principle applies to the selection of models as the following idea: among all the models that may be selected, the well-known data can be well explained and it is very simple to be the best model, that is, the model that should be selected. From the perspective of Bayesian estimation, this can be easily explained as hard as it is to implement. It can be assumed that a complex model has a large prior probability, and a simple model has a small prior probability.

So usually we use L1-norm and L2-norm as regularization terms.

L1-norm

This is the basic norm of machine learning applications. When the L1-norm is used as a regularization term to constrain the parameters; our optimization problem can be written. The LaGrange multiplier method can be used to merge the constraints into the optimization function.

Among them, the constants corresponding to one- to-one is used to weigh the error term and the regularization term. The larger the constraint, the stronger the constraint. In the two-dimensional case, the contour map of the loss function and the L1-norm regularization constraint are respectively drawn under the same coordinate axis.

The L1-norm constraint corresponds to a square norm ball on the plane. The place where the contour line intersects the norm ball for the first time is the optimal solution. It can be seen that the L1-ball has a "corner" where it intersects each coordinate axis, and most of the time the contour line intersects the norm ball at the corner. Such a partial parameter value is set to 0, which is equivalent to the feature corresponding to the parameter will no longer function, the feature selection is realized, and the interpretability of the model is increased.

Regarding the regularization of L1-norm, it can be explained as follows: the trained parameters represent weights and reflect the importance of features. For example, the characteristics are more important than the changes, because the changes will bring more change. In the artificially selected features, there are often some redundant features or useless features. L1-norm regularization resets the weights of these features to 0, which realizes feature selection and simplifies the model. The L1-norm has an inflection point at x=0, so the analytical solution cannot be directly obtained, and the non-conductive convex function needs to be processed by the sub gradient method.

L2-norm

In addition to the L1-norm, there is a widely used regularization norm. This mostly deals with complex characteristics like modulus.

When the L2-norm is used as a regularization term to constrain the parameters, our optimization problem can be written

You can also merge the constraints into the optimization function to get the following function. Also, plot the contour plot of the loss function and the L2-norm regularization constraint on the same coordinate axis.

The L2-norm constraint corresponds to a circular norm ball on the plane. The place where the contour line intersects the norm ball for the first time is the optimal solution. Unlike the L1-norm, the L2-norm is such that each is small, close to 0, but not equal to 0, and the L2-norm regularization still attempts to use each dimension feature. The L2-norm regularization can be explained as follows.

The L2-norm regularization term limits the parameters to a smaller range. The smaller the parameter, the smoother the surface, so it does not appear in a small interval, and the curvature is large. In the case of a large change, it will only change a little bit, and the model is, therefore, more stable, which is more generalization. After adding the L2-norm regularization term, the objective function expands to the following.

Similarly, if the least-squares method is used, the form of the normal equation needs to be modified accordingly, and when the number of samples is less than the dimension of the feature, the matrix will be less than the rank and irreversible. Specifically, the equations are indefinite equations. There will be infinite solutions. The existing data is not enough to determine a solution. In mathematics, constraints are often added to make the unique solution possible. Adding the L2-norm regularization term corresponds to this method.

The explanation about the regularization of L1-norm and L2-norm is the summary of the individual, and there may be inaccuracies. I hope everyone will not hesitate to enlighten me.

Implementation in python:

```
# Parameters initialization
initial_beta = np.ones((Y.shape[2], 2))
#Turn lambda to 2
Lambda = 2
#Use regularization principles
function, grad=costFunction(initial_beta, Y, z,
Lambda)print("Beta (zeros):," function)
```

In the machine learning process, in order to find the best generalization performance of that function, we need to determine the parameters of two aspects:

1) Assuming the function parameters, that is, we usually refer to and, through a variety of parameters such optimization algorithm Automatically obtained.

2) Model parameters, such as the number of polynomials in polynomial regression, regularization parameters, etc. These parameters are called hyperparameters and are usually specified manually before the model training (of course, algorithms such as grid method can also be used for optimization). The process of determining model hyperparameters is called model selection.

Now we need to determine the number of polynomial regressions. We manually assign values from 1 to 10 then use this to train different varied models and find the optimal parameters, and then evaluate the performance of the model on the test set to get the test error. The one with the smallest test error is taken as the optimal model, assuming that we have chosen the model.

Now that the problem is coming, how do we evaluate the generalization performance of this model? Still using test error? If we use the test error as a measure, then can we continue to adjust the value until the test error is minimized, but can we believe the model at this time? Obviously, it is unbelievable, because we have already seen the test data in advance, and our hyperparameters are set around better fitting test data, so it is likely to be an optimal estimate of generalization error.

The problem is that we use the test data multiple times, and the violation of the test data is only a principle for evaluating the function that is built for natural theory. This can be solved using the following strategy such as using a piece in the training set. As a basis for model selection, we call this part of the data a verification set. Now our data set is composed of two parts: The first training set and the set that is used that is the test set.

Training Set: This can be explicitly used to calculate the sum which is very difficult to attain otherwise.

Verification Set: This is basically the same if it is used to get the hyperparameter turning into action.

Test Set: Used only for performance evaluation of trained optimal functions.

The training set, the verification set, and the test set are clearly defined, and each should be replaced by another. In particular, you can't confuse the validation set with the test set.

Again, the data that evaluates the performance of the function that is ultimately learned is called a test set. The test set must be completely independent. The test set should be archived until the model adjustment and parameter training are completed. Use the test set in any form. Information is a spy.

Therefore, the whole process of machine learning at this time is as follows:

1) Determine a set of hyperparameters for the model
2) Train the model with the training set and find the optimal function that minimizes the loss function.
3) This can be validated using a function and easily verified. Repeat steps 1, 2, and 3 until you have searched for the specified hyperparameter combination.

Select the model with the smallest error on the verification set and can be used to verify various other defined and characteristic models to find the optimal function. This can be easily applied and used when it is based on a test set that can be easily analyzed and declared to be used for model paramotoring.

Finally, we all know that the functions that the same model learns on different training sets tend to be different. How do we guarantee that the selected models and functions are the best? Rather than just a special case of current data partitioning? The Cross-Validation method can be used. The basic idea is as follows: divide the training set into K parts, use different K1 to analyze the problems and necessity of the K errors on the set. As the error of the model.

In this chapter, we have learned in a very solid amount about how to fit data into a model for better results. We will use this knowledge to further expand using cost function optimization and gradient descent in the next chapter.

Chapter 4: Cost function optimization

This chapter will introduce some macro core concepts and measures to evaluate the performance of classification algorithms and classifiers, especially how to evaluate some errors in classifier prediction. This is in detail known as cost function optimization.

False Positives and False Positives

The first is the false positive and false negative and can be used to define basic concepts. Returning to the previous example of logistic regression, the sigmoid function is shown below to predict whether something will happen, such as whether the user will purchase the product.

We treat a probability of less than 0.5 as not buying, and users over 0.5 will buy it. Suppose now that four users are known, 13 are not purchased, and 24 are purchased. But we can still use the classifier to try to predict the result.

When we project the data points onto the avatar, we will find two different errors. For the error of user No. 3, we call it a false positive, or a type 1 error. For error No. 2, we call it a false negative or a type 2 error. error. In general, type 2 errors are much more serious than type 1 errors. For example, to judge AIDS, suppose that if we judge that a person without a disease is positive, this result has a certain degree of seriousness, but will be tested again and finally resolved. However, if it is actually a carrier of the virus but is judged to be negative, the result is relatively more serious because it may delay the treatment of the disease.

Confusion Matrix

The confusion matrix has been mentioned in previous articles, and I will explain it here. As shown in the figure below, the horizontal axis refers to the actual value and the vertical axis represents the predicted value.

35 represents the number of actual values is 0, our prediction is also 0, 50 refers to the number of actual 1 prediction is also 1. Obviously, it can be seen here that they both represent varied variable distinctions and can be solved easily. At this point, two ratios can be obtained,

one is the correct rate, that is, the correct number of judgments 35 + 50 = 85 this can be easily calculated using the options we have and the errors 10 + 5 = 15 divided by other numbers that consist of different numbers.

Accuracy paradox

Sometimes these two ratios in the confusion matrix do not indicate too much problem, and sometimes more advanced methods are needed to evaluate the quality of the classifier.

Obviously, it can be calculated that the correct rate is equal to 98%. Does it mean that the quality of this classifier is very good? Now we give a new classification method, no matter what data is raised, it is predicted to be 0. It is equivalent to the number in the right column is added to the left column. Now calculate the accuracy, you will find that the accuracy rate has become 98.5%. That is to say, although the method used is very simple and rude, the actual accuracy is better than the previous one. This shows that in this way it is not suitable for judging the results of a classification in this scenario, and other better methods are needed.

Cumulative Accuracy Profile

In the above case, it can be seen that the quality of the classification result is sometimes not well judged by the confusion matrix. Now let's look at a more advanced judgment method called the cumulative accuracy curve (CAP). Let's look at the example below. The traverse is the customer we contact, and the vertical axis is the number of customers we buy.

Then we can get a straight line. These customers are all customers who are connected by our random sampling. At this point, suppose we use a well-trained algorithm to determine whether the user will buy the product. After getting the predicted result, we can give priority to the customer who will buy the product, so that the customer we just started will have a high probability. Will buy products, as the number of contacts increases, such as to 60,000, the prediction of the remaining people will not buy products, from the company's point of view, in fact, you cannot contact the remaining customers, because they bought the probability is relatively small. But here to draw the curve completely, continue to draw the points behind. That is to say, no matter what kind of model is used, when we completely contact all customer groups, that is, 100,000 customers, the last point must be coincident.

Obviously, this curve is above the previous image because we used machine learning algorithms to make the company's operations more efficient. The better the model, the more convex the model will be. Now change the value on the horizontal and vertical axes to a percentage. 100% of the horizontal axis refers to the 100% customer base, and 100% of the vertical axis refers to the estimated total number of users who will purchase.

Suppose there is another model now, and no red model is good. Then its possible image will be like the green curve above because if you use a better model, then the number of users actually buying at a certain point should be relatively high. When compared to other matrixes we can easily say that either this model is good or bad by using different scenarios. Suppose there is a very good model at this time, we call it Crystal Ball, what would this image look like? We used to know that about 10,000 people in 10,000 would buy products, that is, 10% would buy them. The best model is to find this 10 % from the beginning.

The black line above shows the apex of the image at 10%, followed by a line parallel to the horizontal axis. This model can be said to be the most perfect model, almost impossible to achieve, so it is called the crystal ball model. If we have a curve that appears below the blue curve, this shows that the model is not as good as a better prediction, or even as a random sample, which is easier to find.

In addition to the CAP curve, there is a similar curve that can be used in real life, which is called ROC (Receiver Operating Characteristic). You can query the data yourself. Then we know that the red curve in the above picture is closer to the perfect curve to illustrate the better the model. Now let's see how to quantify this kind of good and bad.

Represented by the perfect curve and the blue curve, defined as the area of the machine learning model and the blue curve. Defined at his time the closer the ratio is to 1, the better the model we build. There are already some statistical tools to calculate this ratio. But it's cumbersome to calculate by hand or by machine. By using different conditions and reasons we can understand whether a particular model is good for the usage or not. At this point, a 50% threshold is used, which is to find 50% of the points this can be easily done using different axis methods that are being perpetrated. This point can provide good information.

As shown in the above figure, we divide the value of X into different intervals and give different evaluations when the values of X are located at different intervals. Since the stochastic model reaches 50% at 50%, X<60% indicates that it is not much better than random, and it is judged to be a particularly poor model. A little better is a poor model. Moving on is a good model. As X increases, the model gets better and better.

But when it is more than 90%, this model is exaggerated, and attention should be paid at this time. This is not the result we want. In the first case, a different dependent variable should be given to understand the complexity such as the number of calls with the user, this has a very strong causal relationship, then this feature needs to be taken from our self excluded from the variable. The second case is over-fitting, which means that the model pays too much attention to the noise in the training set, which is also a concern. However, there are some cases where more than 90% are located because the training set is of very high quality, or the model built is very good.

Classification algorithm summary

There are currently six classification algorithms, and the following is a summary of the advantages and disadvantages of each classification model

For different cases, how to choose a model, the first step is to judge whether linear or nonlinear:

- If it is a linear problem, you should choose logistic regression or support vector machine SVM.
- If it is a nonlinear problem, you should choose naive Bayes, decision trees or random forests. In the next lesson, we will talk about the neural network, which is also a very powerful method.

There are also some rules from the perspective of actual operation:

- If you want to rank the final predicted probability, you should choose either logistic regression or Naive Bayes. For example, you want to predict the probability of different customers buying a product and sort these probabilities from large too small to target the target customer base. In such cases, if your problem is linear, you should use logistic regression; if your problem is non-linear, you should choose the naive Bayes model.
- If you want to predict which segment each customer belongs to, you should choose SVM. The division of the market and customer groups can be

the result of completed market research or clustering.

- If you want to show/declare the model very intuitively, then the Decision Tree is the best choice.
- If you want the best model classification and don't care much about the model's presentation/explanation, a random forest is a good choice.

The above is the basic knowledge of the performance evaluation and selection of the classification model.

Gradient descent and least squares

The Regression model means that the output of the function learned by the machine learning method is a continuous real value, and the regression model can be used for prediction or classification. This section mainly includes linear regression models and polynomial regression models for prediction.

Linear regression

According to the three steps of machine learning modeling, we first need to determine the model chosen, here is the Linear regression model, and then formally express it. Among them, is the n-dimensional attribute description of the sample data, each group and can determine a different, and all combinations of values constitute an optional function set, our task is to select the most from this function set that's a good function.

The training data set D is described as follows: where is the n-dimensional eigenvector representation of the sample, which is the sample marker. The goal of linear regression is to learn a linear function to predict the real value output markers as accurately as possible. Therefore, we need to determine a metric to measure the quality of a function, that is, choose the appropriate loss function (Loss Function). According to the goal of linear regression, we only need to measure the difference between the mean and the mean square error (MSE) is the most commonly used loss function in the regression task.

Because it is a function, the above formula can also be written. The smallest function that can be made is the best function we are looking for. Now we need to choose an optimization algorithm to find out from many. The commonly used methods are Gradient Descent and Least Square Method

Gradient Descent

Partial derivatives are obtained for each variable of the multivariate function, and the result is written as a vector form, which is a gradient. For example, the function, respectively, is to find the partial derivative, which is the gradient. Geometrically, the gradient is the fastest direction of the function at that point, so it is easier to get a minimum resulted in from a function that can be used to get a lot of basic numerical things of the gradient. The below is an intuitive explanation of the gradient descent.

For example, we want to reach the foot of a mountain at a certain position in a mountain. Since we don't know how to go down the mountain we can use this negative function to determine the complexity of gradient descent and how they can be used. That is, the current steepest direction goes down until it reaches the position where the gradient is zero. Of course, if you go on like this, you may not be able to walk to the foot of the mountain, but to a low point in a local mountain.

Therefore, the gradient descent does not necessarily find the global optimal solution and maybe a locally optimal solution. If the loss function is a convex function, the gradient descent algorithm will certainly find the global optimal solution.

The steps of the gradient descent algorithm are as follows:

1) Select an initial value by using different random sampling methods.

2) Calculate, where is the learning rate, which determines the step size for each adjustment

3) Iterate the second step multiple times until the gradient is zero, or the loss reaches the allowable range, or the number of iterations is reached.

Least-squares

The least-squares method can also be used to estimate the pair, and the least-squares method directly solves the analytical solution. For the sake of discussion, we combine the components into a vector and add a constant attribute value of 1 to each sample. The data set that is basically used which is E is represented as a matrix of one size.

Then mark the mark as a vector form, then there is similarly= (y1; y2; ⋯ ; ym)y=(y1;y2;⋯;ym).

Loss function

Let the above formula be equal to zero, and the closed solution of the optimal solution can be obtained. Which is the inverse matrix, there may not full rank matrix, a common practice is to introduce regularization (regularization) items.

Advantages and disadvantages of gradient descent and least squares

1. The gradient descent algorithm is applicable to all optimization problems, but the least squares method is only applicable to linear problems. When the regression model is not a linear model, it needs to be converted to

linear by some techniques to use the least squares method.

2. The least squares method needs to be solved. There may be cases where the matrix does not have an inverse matrix. In this case, it is necessary to add regularization term or delete some redundant features, let the determinant not be 0, and then continue to use the least squares method. In addition, when the sample size is large, solving the inverse matrix will be a very time-consuming process, and using the gradient descent algorithm will be advantageous.

3. When the sample data is not very large and there is an analytical solution, the least squares method is faster than the gradient descent algorithm.

Polynomial regression

Some sample data may not be particularly suitable when fitted with linear regression. At this time, you can try to use polynomial regression. As shown in the following figure, it is a sample data set of house price and house area. It can be clearly found that all data points are not distributed in a certain near a straight line, you can consider trying quadratic or cubic functions at this time.

For polynomial regression, it can also be regarded as a new attribute. Polynomial regression is the same as linear regression, so the training method of polynomial regression is still the same as linear regression. It should be noted that you should not choose a relatively complex polynomial model when you can choose a simple linear model.$x2, x3$

In detail about Gradient descent

Gradient Descent is the most commonly used optimization method when training machine learning models to find optimal functions. Given a set of initial parameters, the gradient descent algorithm can gradually approach the lowest point, which is the position of the best parameter, along the direction in which the loss function drops the fastest. Why is the gradient descent algorithm work? Why is the opposite direction of the gradient the fastest way to reduce the loss function?

Gradient descent algorithm explanation

First, let's review of how the gradient descent algorithm works. Our goal is to find:

Among them is the loss function, the gradient descent algorithm steps are as follows:

1) A set of initial parameters is randomly selected.
2) Calculate the partial derivative of the loss function at that point, which is the gradient.
3) Update parameters.

Repeat steps 2 and 3 until the gradient no longer drops (less than a certain threshold range).

As you can see in step 3 above, each time we update in the opposite direction of the gradient, which is the learning rate, represents the size of each update. The intuitive process of gradient descent when there are only two unknown parameters is shown below:

The following explains the principle of gradient descent according to the idea of Li Hongyi's course. Also, assume that there are only two parameters, Randomly give an initial point, looking for the direction in which the loss function drops the fastest in the range of "what is within."

Implementation of the gradient descent in python:

```
def      gradientdescentfunction(Y,z,Theta,rateoflearning
=0.02, iterations =50)

# Y = Matrix with bias units
z = Vector of Z
iterations = number of iterations that are present


n = len(z)
historyofcost = np.zero(iterations)


prediction = np.dot(z,Theta)
cost_history = cal_cost(theta,Z,y)
```

return theta,historyofcost,historyoftheta

Some tips for gradient descent

1) Learning rate (learning rate)

The learning rate is a hyperparameter that needs to be adjusted most. Too small will make the training speed too slow; too much will make the training unable to converge, so it is necessary to adjust the learning rate very carefully.

We can plot the loss function as shown on the left side of the figure. The red learning rate is the most appropriate, the blue is too small, the green is too large, and the yellow is very large. However, when the number of parameters is large, the loss function curve cannot be visualized. At this time, we can plot the loss value curve with the number of iterations, as shown . If the loss drops very slowly (blue), the learning rate may be too low; if the loss begins to fall very quickly but quickly stabilizes at a large value (green), the learning rate may be too large; if the loss does not fall back (Yellow), the learning rate may be too large; only the loss is reduced to a small (red) at the right speed, which is the best learning rate.

2) Adagrad

Everyone has an intuitive idea: when the initial distance is far away, give a larger learning rate, causing the loss to drop rapidly; when approaching the lowest point, give a smaller learning rate and ensure that the lowest point is reached.

At each iteration, all parameters are given the same size parameters, which may still be not fine enough. It can be easily understood and self-learned because it is changed gradually within the prescribed time. Adagrad is the most commonly used method, and the learning which is easily described is divided into various parameters that cannot be learned or known again.

3. Stochastic Gradient Descent or Mini-Batch Gradient Descent

It is the partial derivative on the whole data set. In this method, we need to calculate the error of each sample point in the whole data set for each update, so the speed will be slower. The data set, the memory may not be able to accommodate and cannot be used, so in practice, generally, you need to use these systems to attain great knowledge over the sample space when compared to other systems.

Each update of the Stochastic Gradient Descent calculates the loss function for every sample that is used to improve the model we can learn using different quantitative methods and the batch gradient is updated once and the SGD can be updated m times, although each time Considering only one sample point, there may be large fluctuations, but eventually it will converge. This min batch can be used to vary or improvise the gradient descent functions using different innumerable applications. For each update, the loss function is calculated for some data in the data set.

4. Feature scaling

The value range on the left side of the figure is one percent. When there is a slight change, the value will vary greatly, so the loss function will also change greatly, that is, the loss function will drop rapidly in the direction, resulting in the loss function contour. The line is flat and elliptical. In this case, it is more difficult to deal with without Adagrad, and different learning rates are required in both directions. However, after the feature is scaled, the range of values of all features is uniform, and the contour of the loss function is a regular circle, and the gradient descent efficiency will be relatively high.

In this chapter, we learned in detailed about gradient descent and its implementation using python. In the next chapter, we will start going to discuss data preprocessing methods like data cleansing for diving into data science journey. Follow up for further knowledge.

Chapter 5: Handling, Cleaning and Preparing Data

Data preprocessing is a very important step in machine learning. In order to analyze the data correctly and get the best machine learning algorithm, we generally need to preprocess the data after getting the data. Data preprocessing involves the following steps:

1. Import data set
2. Handling missing data
3. Classification data
4. Data is successfully divided into two called as training and test
5. Feature scaling

Import data set

This set of data reflects the influence of the user's nationality, age, and salary on whether or not to purchase the product. Importing datasets, we generally use the panda's package. For this set of data, the first three columns are independent variables, and the last column is the dependent variable, which is the result we want to predict. Then the code to be used for implementation can be as described as below (here we first import the package to be used later):

```
import pandas as some variable
from themodule.selectedmodel
import splittraintest
from themodule.processbefore
 import Standardpath = '../place/place.csv'
#import the dataset as follows
dataset = pd.place_csv(standardpath)
X = dataset.prescr[0,-1].values
y = dataset.prescr[1,3].values
```

The variables all data except the last column of all rows in the data and y is the result of the last column. In this way, the data set is imported.

Handling missing data

Looking closely at this set of data sets, we will find that there are several rows of data with missing data. For example, the fifth line of data lacks information on salary.

So, what should I do with this missing data? There are two ways to do this:

- Delete missing data (simple operation but high risk, easy to delete important data)
- Take the average of the column instead of missing data

So how to deal with python, we need to use a powerful sklearn package, which Imputer class can be used to process missing data, the code is as follows:

```
#This will take care of data that is missed
from themodule.beforeprocessing
import presentvalue = presentvalue(values missed =
'DnD', strategy = 'mode', presence = 2)
presentvalue= presentvalue.presence(X[0, 1,3])X[-1, 1,3]
= presentvalue.change(X[0, 1,3])
```

After processing, we will look at the data of X and find that the missing data has been filled by the average of the column.

Classification Data

Careful observation of this set of data is a numerical value for both age and salary, while the country is a category for each country. Whether to buy or not only buy and not buy two categories. In machine learning, we essentially use equations to process data differently. For this different category, we need to convert it into different values to bring us into our equations. In Python, the sklearn package is still used. The tool to be used is the Label Encoder. code show as below:

```
# This is a label encoder problem that needs to be
learned
Encode datavalue
import module.processing
import nameofencoder
Xencoder = callthefunction()
Yencoder = callthefunction()
Hotencoder = categorical[result]
```

After we use Label Encoder for conversion, the first column of data will turn the country into 0, 1, 2, but this will bring a problem, originally these countries only represent different categories, but after converting to numbers They will be unintentionally sorted, and these sorts are meaningless, so **virtual coding is** used here to solve this problem.

The so-called virtual coding, as shown in the following figure, the nationality of the original data has three categories of France, Spain, and Germany, then we can divide it into three columns, each column represents whether the user is a group of this column, for example, if the user is France People, then the French column is 1, and the other two columns are 0.

Using virtual coding, you can change the original column of variables into three columns of variables, but there is no order difference between the values. The tool used here is OneHotEncoder, the code is also given above, and categorical features refers to which column to process. Of course, don't forget the last column. Since the last column is a dependent variable, Python's function can automatically identify this column as categorical data, so you don't need to use OneHotEncoder and directly use Label Encoder.

Data is divided into training sets and test sets

As we already discussed before splitting we need to talk about what is the training set and the test set. First, let's talk about the meaning of the term machine learning. Machine learning, as the name implies, is to let the machine learn the relationship between the data, and can use the learned results to predict the new data. Then the process of learning is to constantly modify the formula through the data. The machine learns the relevance of the data from the data in the training set. After learning, the machine needs to test the results of its training in the new data, the test set. In Python, there is a very simple way to split a dataset like this.

#Splitting using techniques

usetest1, usetest2, usetest3, usetest4 = splitthedata(first, second, sizeoftest = 0.4, random_state = 0)

Test_size refers to the proportion of the test set, the last random_state refers to the split method, the same random_state cut out the same result.

Feature scaling

Looking back at this set of data, the focus here is on the age and salary. The age value is basically floating at 30-50, while the salary is floating between 50,000 and 80,000. There is a term in machine learning called **Euclidean distance**. The so-called Euclidean distance can be regarded as the distance between two points in the plane. Obviously, the sum of the squares of the horizontal and vertical coordinate differences is added and then squared.

Then the question comes. If the salary and age here are the horizontal and vertical coordinates, then the square of the coordinate difference of the salary is very large compared with the age, then the effect of age on this result will become very small. Therefore, we need to scale the age and salary to the same order of magnitude. Some algorithms may not use Euclidean distance, but after feature scaling, the convergence speed of the algorithm will be much faster (such as decision tree).

Next, let's look at how to feature scaling. There are two algorithms:

Standardization and Normalization

In the standardization, mean one need to understand the basis of other examples and remaining used cases need to represents the standard deviation, that is, how much floatingness is measured in a column of data. What is obtained here is the distribution with an average of 0 and a variance of 1.

The code in python looks like this:

```
#This describes the scaling method
secondvalue= scalingfunction()
firstvariable= secondvalue.makethistransform(firstvalue)
firstvalue= scaling
first.transform(testvalue)
```

Remember that in the above classification data, the first column and the last column are both virtual coded. Do these virtual variables need to be feature-scaled? This needs to be analyzed for different scenarios.

The values of the variables here are only 0 and 1, it looks Feature scaling has been performed, so feature scaling can be omitted, but the performance of the algorithm may be improved after feature scaling, and feature scaling is performed here. After the feature is scaled by the independent variable, look at the dependent variable, where the dependent variable represents a different category, so there is no need here. If it is a regression problem, the dependent variable may need to be scaled.

Classification Problem

This section will introduce another important task in machine learning - classification, that is, find a function to determine the category to which the input data belongs, which can be a two-category problem (yes/no) or a multi-category problem (It is judged among a plurality of categories which category the input data specifically belongs to).

Compared to the regression problem, the output of the classification problem is no longer a continuous value, but a discrete value that specifies which category it belongs to. Classification problems are widely used in reality, such as spam recognition, handwritten digit recognition, face recognition, and speech recognition.

Thinking

First, think about a question, can you solve the classification problem with the solution to the regression problem?

Taking the two-category problem as an example, for category 1 we make things assume that the constant value in 1 and for category 2 understand the constant value is one that cannot be defined. In the regression problem, we need to understand what needs to be thought of as undefined when compared to the target. For the sake of easy understanding, it is assumed that each sample is represented by only two-dimensional features.

At this point, the points in the lower right corner are added to category 1. If the function represented by the green line is still used for prediction, the error of these newly added points will be particularly large, in order to alleviate the error caused by this. The green line will be offset to the lower right corner to reduce the error. However, it is obviously unreasonable to do so.

Although the error is reduced, it also brings more serious classification category errors. The essence of this problem is the inappropriate definition of the loss function. The regression problem locates the loss function as the error function because the goal of the regression is to fit the sample points as much as possible, but the goal of the classification problem is to classify the sample points as correct as possible. In the category, it is obviously not appropriate to use the error function as a loss function.

There will be such a joke: for those points with obvious categories, the punishment for solving the regression problem is even more serious. In addition, for the multi-category problem, we assign a corresponding target value to each category. In the machine's view, these target values are related. For example, the category 1 target value is specified as 1, and the category 2 target value is specified as 2 The category 3 target value is specified as 3... When the computer is looking for a relationship between samples, the default category 2 and category 3 are more relevant than category 1 and category 3 because 3 and 2 are closed.

In this chapter, we have a brief understanding of data preprocessing methods and in the next chapters, we will deal about future engineering and feature selection that will help to further understand the subject in detail.

Chapter 6: Feature Engineering and Feature

Selection

In real-world scenarios, we now have access to a lot of data. Data which is messy, unorganized, non-linear and often complex that cannot be used without a proper strategy or methodology. To implement a successful machine learning model we need this data to be turned into a piece of valuable information that further can be used or mastered in a way such that it can turn into a valuable insight that can solve real world problems.

Importance of Valuable data

Nowadays every technological company, for example, Google, Amazon or even budding startups collect their user data to utilize or train their machine learning algorithms. No one can deny the fact that Data is valuable and important for artificial intelligence and its predecessors. Often data that is collected is messy and can take hundreds of days (sometimes years even) to interpret them. If we can understand where the data is coming interpretation can become simple.

Understanding Data

Data we deal with can be of different types as described below.

1) Numerical data

This type of data deals with numerical measurements i.e quantitative data. Weight or age of people, Stock value of Amazon, Performance rate of a website, etc., come under this category. Numerical data can be further divided into two types as explained below.

a) Discrete Data:

This data deals with integer values and can often give information about a particular event.

Example:

Number of bookmarked songs for a particular Spotify user.

b) Continuous Data:

This deals with different values that can be possessed for a single entity.

Example:

Delivery time for two different Amazon products falls under continuous data.

2) Categorical Data

Internet is filled with categorical data due to its easy integration in web applications. They are data without any mathematical relation or significance.

Example: Type of country in a data form , Sex, Nationality, etc.

3) Ordinal Data

Ordinal data just mixes up both numerical and categorical data where its categorical entities possess a mathematical value.

Example:

A user rating for a movie, Car ride or a restaurant.

When we understand data better, we can get the confidence to monitor and improve those using different methods of Feature engineering. We will look about it in the next section in detail.

What is feature engineering?

In the machine learning industry people who are just trying to get into it always gets confused with one basic thing that is sensing that data and its characteristics are the most important entity unlike models and other well-distinguished algorithms that we usually concentrate more. Always try to get sensible and useful data that can be trained vigorously to get our desired results or expectations easily. We use future engineering techniques for the same purpose to turn any unreliable data into useful and successful data that can be used in a lot of software testing models and applications to solve real world problems.

Feature selection has two main purposes:

- Reduce feature quantity and dimension reduction, make the model generalization ability stronger, and reduce over-fitting;
- Enhance understanding between features and eigenvalues.

Feature processing is one of the most utilized or talked feature engineering subsets. This basically gives models or strategies that can be used to make the data applicable to a lot of models and use them to train and acquire desired results. Scikitlearn which we use in this chapter also gives a lot of modules or libraries that can be used to polish data. There are functions for selecting the data and using certain dimensional reduction methods to get the data-rich and handle them using various other techniques.

Exploratory analysis can better understand the data set, examine the characteristics and shape of the data set, verify some of the ideas in the mind, and have a preliminary idea of the next steps in the data task.

Here I used the local iris dataset, the method is the same, there is no difference, the attention is that you need to look at the form of the data and the header in the loading process does not need to be loaded.

Filter

The main idea of the filtering method is to "score" each feature according to divergence or correlation, that is, to give weight to each dimension, such weight represents the importance of the feature. Set the threshold or the number of thresholds to be selected and select the feature.

Removing Features with Low Variance

This should be the simplest feature selection method: suppose the eigenvalues of a feature are only 0 and 1, and in all input samples, 95% of the instances have a value of 1, then it can be considered that this feature does not work. Big. If 100% is 1, then this feature is meaningless. This method can be used when the eigenvalues are discrete variables.

If it is a continuous variable, the continuous variables need to be discretized before they can be used. In practice, generally, 95% or more will take a certain value. The characteristics exist, so this method is simple but not very useful. It can be used as a pre-processing for feature selection. First, the features with small changes in value are removed, and then the appropriate feature selection is selected from the feature selection methods mentioned below for further feature selection.

Using the variance selection method, the variance of each feature is first calculated, and then the feature whose variance is greater than the threshold is selected according to the threshold.

In this chapter, we had a brief discussion about the methods of feature engineering and feature selection. We even tried to further improve your knowledge by using different examples. In the next chapter, we will discuss cross-validation in detail.

Chapter 7: Cross-validation

Cross-Validation

When training machine learning models, we hope to get a model with excellent generalization performance. In the previous blog regression model, when we used polynomial regression and increased the number of polynomials, the model became more and more complex, but the error on the test set did not gradually decrease.

This shows that a complex model does not always show better performance on the test set. So, where does the error come from?

Generalization error

We know that the results learned by the algorithm on different training sets are likely to be different, even if the training sets are from the same distribution. To return to the task, for example, the test sample, so as marked on the data set for the real mark, due to the presence of noise, it is possible, and as in the training set school was a function of the predicted output. Therefore, the expected prediction of the algorithm can be expressed.

The variance of the predicted output of the function learned by different training, the difference between the expected output and the true mark is called the bias, the expected generalization error of the algorithm. Wherein the first equation is equal to 0 and red, as with independent, so that, depending on the desired prediction formulas have . Similarly, the second red-added formula is equal to 0 because the noise expectation is zero. Noise can't be artificially controlled, so usually, we think.

$$E(f; D) = bias2(x) + var(x)$$
$$E(f;D)=bias2(x)+var(x)$$

Now that you know where the generalization error comes from, you need to do targeted control.

Bias and variance

According to the above definition, the bias reflects the difference between the expected output of the model on the sample and the true mark, that is, the accuracy of the model itself, reflecting the fitting ability of the model itself. The variance reflects the error between the output of the function learned by the model under different training data sets and the expected output, ie the stability of the model, and the fluctuation of the model. The deviation and variance are visually shown below using the example of shooting.

The red bull' s eye represents the true mark of the test sample, and the blue dots represent the output of the function selected by the model on different training sets. In the two graphs in the first column, the blue points are concentrated, indicating that the stability of the model is good, that is, the variance is small; in the two graphs of the first row, the center of the blue dot is closer to the red bull's-eye, indicating The model has a strong ability to fit, that is, the deviation is small. So summarized as follows:

1) Low and Low variance BIAS: steady and accurate and

2) Low bias and high variance: quasi-unstable but

3) High bias and low variance: not allowed but stable

4) High bias and high variance: they are not allowed to instability

That model and deviation, what is the correspondence between variances, take the regression task as an example. Looking at an extreme example, no matter how the training data of the model changes, the learned function will not change, so the output is the same, that is, the stability of the model is very good, but the training set is proposed.

The combination is not very good. Obviously, the prediction of the test sample will not be very accurate. This case of insufficient training of the training set is called underfitting. Gradually increase the complexity of the model, and the learned function fits the training data better and better.

However, for a complex model, when we change the training sample slightly, the learned function gap will be very large.

This shows that the complex model fits well on the training samples, but the volatility of the model is also very large, and it is very likely that the performance of the test samples is very poor. It can be understood that a complex model takes the characteristics of the training sample as the generality of the whole sample and introduces noise into the model. This phenomenon is called overfitting. So, we need to weigh the complexity of the model so that the deviation and variance are traded off so that the overall error of the model is minimal.

Under-fitting and over-fitting coping strategies
Under-fitting (not enough)

1) Find better features and improve your ability to portray data
2) Increase the number of features
3) Reselect more complex models

4) Overfitting (the characterization is too thin, the generalization is too poor)

5) Increase the samples may increase the noise too in some cases.

6) Reduce feature dimension, low dimensional density

7) Add regularization to make the model smoother

Model selection

The functions that the same model learns on different training sets tend to be different. How can we choose the best model and the best function? The Cross-Validation method can be used. The basic idea is as follows: this can be regularized into K parts, each time using K-1 parts like this can be used to be used for training sets, the error is then calculated on the validation set. The above process is repeated again by selecting another K-1 data. The error can be exchanged and can be used for various other reasons, and the best model is selected according to this value. Finally, the best selection of training is used to apply on other various different models that cannot be divided.

At the same time, cross-validation also solves the above two problems of variance (the difference between the functions learned by different training sets) and bias (the average of different functions). To put it bluntly, cross-validation verifies that your model is accurate enough and stable enough. It can't be said that it works well on a certain dataset. The model you make is to be placed on the entire dataset. After all, the generalization ability is It is the core of machine learning.

Overview

In experimental data analysis, some algorithms need to build models with existing data, such as Convolutional Neural Networks (CNN), which is called Supervised Learning. The data needed to build a model is called training data.

After the model is built, you need to use the data to verify the correctness of the model. This part of the data is called test data. Test data cannot be used in the build model and can only be used to verify the accuracy of the model.

Sometimes in the process of building a model, it is also necessary to test the model and assist in model building. Therefore, the training data will be divided into two parts, 1) training data; 2) verification data.

To classify data, cross-validation is required. The cross-validation algorithm written by individuals is inevitably flawed. Consider using a powerful sklearn package to implement cross-validation algorithms.

Python implementation

Please note: The following method implementations are implemented according to the latest sklearn version, and many of the older versions of the functions have expired.

K-Fold Cross-Validation

The general idea of the K-cross-check is to roughly divide the data into K sub-samples, one sample at a time as verification data, and take the remaining K-1 samples as training data.

```
from importthedatvalue

from importthemodule

from skikitlearn

#This can be used to import

#create array in this step

X = np.array[[32,44],[x,y],[m,n]]

kfold = model(that describes the function)

kfold(array.X,inverse)

model = Test(kfold.X)

index = model(array)

result:

print (output)

else

null or exit
```

Output :

a

b

c

d

e

Stratified k-fold

The StratifiedKFold() function is more commonly used. The advantage of KFold is that the K-fold data is divided into data sets according to the percentage. The percentage of each category is the same in the training set and the test set so that there is no certain category of data to be trained. Concentration does not have this situation in the test set, nor does it not have a full test set in the training set, which can lead to a terrible result.

```
from importthedatvalue
from importthemodule
from skikitlearn
from import stratified
#This can be used to import
#create array in this step
X = np.array[[32,44],[x,y],[m,n]]
stratifiedkfold = model(that describes the function)
stratifiedkfold(array.X,inverse)
model = Test(stratifiedkfold.X)
index = model(array)
result:
```

```
print (output)
else
null or exit
```

Output :

```
x
y
z
w
u
v
```

Train_test_split

The training set and test set are randomly assigned according to the scale. This function can adjust the random seed.

```
from importthedatvalue
from importthemodule
from skikitlearn
#This can be used to import
#create array in this step
```

```
X = np.array[[32,44],[x,y],[m,n]]
traintest = model(that describes the function)
traintest(array.X,inverse)
model = trainTest(kfold.X)
index = model(array)
result:
print (output)
else
null or exit
```

Output:

1

2

3

4

5

6

More cross validation functions available

The sklearn feature is very powerful and provides a lot of cross-validation functions, such as:

1) Base cross validator

We can validate the base cross with this function.

2) Kfold

This can be used for clustering algorithms.

3) Timeseriessplit

This is famously known to be used in time series functions.

4) GridsearchCV

These are used in dimensionality reduction functions.

5) Parameter grid

These are used in grid functions.

6) Shuffle split

These are used in split functions that can be shuffled using various techniques.

7)fit_grid_point

This can be used to fit various grid points.

8) Train_test_split

This can be used to test a train split.

9)Validation_curve

This can be used to visualize curves that can function data.

10) Learning_curve

This can be used to know more about pin-point data.

11) Check_cv

This is a special function that is used for checking cross-validation.

Chapter 8: Challenges in Machine Learning

To this day, we have seen that very accurate machine vision, auditory and voice interactions supported by machine learning algorithms are being applied to a variety of products and services, which in turn has led to explosive growth in AI for commercial applications. But machine learning is still moving forward, and it still has a lot of potentials to wait for us to explore, but only if we can clearly understand the challenges of machine learning today.

Machine learning specialists believe that people now have to deal with a lot of data, which is obviously beyond the scope of human processing, so it needs a computer, and needs more intelligent algorithms that can continuously learn from the data, sum up experience, and continuously improve performance, but include Uncertain factors, systemic risks, and inadequate use of data are all in front of us and are waiting to be resolved.

In the information age, there are many scenes where pain points can be solved by computers. Many of the technologies behind them are connected. Therefore, many application fields are now using machine learning, and more broadly, artificial intelligence. Now, machine learning or artificial intelligence has made significant progress, such as deep learning that everyone is concerned about, including images, speech, and even natural language processing.

We have to deal with a lot of data, which is obviously beyond the scope that people can handle. So, we need computers, we need to be smarter, we can learn from the data, summarize the experience, and continuously improve the performance Algorithm.

Today, in this section mainly wants to share with you that machine learning has developed to the present day. In the case of many applications, we should also think about what kind of problems, or what problems should be solved in future machine learning.

The first challenge we face is what we call uncertainty. These uncertain factors need to be modeled, learned, reasoned, and even finalized when building an artificial intelligence system.

Another challenge is that artificial intelligence solutions or artificial intelligence systems now face some risks, perhaps from an algorithmic perspective or a system perspective. From the algorithm point of view, a well-performing deep neural network can add some noise to this image, but the consequence of this noise is that it can mislead the neural network and give a wrong answer with a very high degree of execution.

These risks are difficult to correct unless you have some other information or people who are helping to correct them.

There are many other shows at the system level, such as the system for displaying face recognition at the 351 parties or the lidar in a driverless car. If you want to destroy it, there are actually many ways, which poses new challenges to the security of the system or algorithm.

There is also the use of data. In the digital world, we have a large amount of data that may not be labeled or have high noise. How to use this data? There are still major deficiencies in the use of these data by our existing methods or existing applications.

But we still have some inspirations, such as AlphaGo, whose latest version can actually generate more data through simulation and simulation to help us guide the training of this algorithm. This idea is more advanced than the frontier. But if you use the actual system but also face a lot of difficulties, a parallel simulation system can be far more complicated than the Go environment.

Everyone is concerned about some recent big plans, such as the recent plan of DAPPA in the United States - AINext, similar to the new generation of artificial intelligence planning made in the UK.

From the point of view of the technology used in our artificial intelligence system, it was used as a basic handwriting detection and writing system in the early days. At this stage, a large amount of learning based on machine learning or machine statistics is required, which requires a huge amount of data that can be traded and delivered.

What is the next stage, they put forward "contextual reasoning," can do reasoning, have a more powerful ability to support many more complex tasks? The main purpose of the five tasks in the specific plan is to continuously improve the complexity and reliability of the problem solved by the artificial intelligence system.

The above are the challenges and future visions of artificial intelligence or machine learning. Let's take a quick look at the attempts and progress in this area.

What progress have we made in the question of modeling, reasoning, and decision making for uncertainty?

In the field of machine learning, there is a special direction called probabilistic machine learning, which mainly includes three levels of work:

At the first level, how can we make it more flexible in the basic theoretical framework of modeling and reasoning, especially how to do friendly modeling when dealing with complex problems.

The second level, the algorithm that can be used to train by using a lot of volume after the model, the algorithm here includes random sampling algorithms, including the use of random gradients in deep learning.

At the third level, large-scale distributed computing and distributed platforms are used for probability calculation.

The second progress is related to robustness and reliability. In the case of malicious attacks or flawed samples in the data, how can we ensure that the system can work according to our preset goals? Actually, there has been a lot of progress and attention recently, including the first international competition held by Google Brain at the NIPS International Conference last year. In fact, it is mainly aimed at confrontation, attack, and defense in deep neural networks. There is also a special competition at the conference about AI Security.

In the latter case, many systems now only have a mapping relationship between input and output. It is difficult to understand how this algorithm or system works. There is a very interesting issue here, called interpretable machine learning, interpretable algorithms, and interpretable systems.

This piece has several levels of work, one that can be used to aid in understanding this method with visual tools, such as deep neural networks. In addition, through the guidance and training in the process of learning, the neurons in the deep neural network can be made more interpretable and closer to the concept of human beings. This can actually introduce some knowledge or semantic information to help us.

The last question - about decision making - decision making is actually a more challenging issue, especially in the case of uncertain environments or incomplete information. For example, the probabilistic method is used to describe the problem of slot machines. In fact, it is typically a game with uncertain information.

In reinforcement learning, related to imitative learning, etc., there has been a lot of progress recently, such as how to do multi-agent cooperation and game in the more complicated scenes such as "StarCraft" and "Knife Tower." There is another international competition in the international arena, a real-time battle game, and how to make intelligent decisions in an unknown environment.

What I mainly want to share with you is that the artificial intelligence now faces some challenges in the actual environment, but the good news is that through long-term exploration, this field is constantly developing, and I hope that artificial intelligence will be better in the future. To solve everyone's problems.

This section in detail explained the challenges that machine learning is facing in the real world. We will further discuss this in detail in the next section.

Chapter 9: Escaping the Curse of Dimensionality

It may seem weird at first when we try to remove features that are not necessary or which are making model predictions irregular. In the previous chapters, we have used future engineering techniques to improve machine learning models whereas now we will take away features that are not necessary or not important for the data. This section will describe more about dimensionality reduction in detail.

So why dimensionality reduction is necessary?
It is a common assumption that more data results in better machine learning end result. But we have several valid reasons that can make us think otherwise that reducing dimensionality is a good strategy for an increase in model performance.

a) Increase in the dimensionality of the data can irritate the learner. A lot of machine learning models perform better when the data have fewer dimensions.

b) When we have high dimensionality feature there is a high chance of overfitting to occur.

c) If you have thought of visualizing available data with different python modules you need to restrict data to two or three dimensions. So, dimensionality reduction is an obvious choice if you want to interpret the data by yourself.

These reasons

1) Methods that can reduce the dimensionality
2) Methods that can reduce the non-dimensionality
3) Autoencoders

Dimensionality Reduction

Dimensionality means that a set of vectors **zi** of d can be used to represent useful information contained in a vector **xi** of number D, where $d < D$. Suppose that for a

512*512 size image, use svm to classify it. The most straightforward approach is to expand the graph into rows or columns into an input vector **xi of** length 512*512 , multiplied by the parameters of svm.

If the vector of 512*512 can be reduced to 100 while retaining useful information, the space for storing input and parameters will be much reduced, and the time for calculating vector multiplication will be much reduced. Therefore, dimensionality reduction can effectively reduce the calculation time. The data in high-dimensional space is likely to be sparsely distributed.

That is, the distribution of 100 samples in 100-dimensional space is definitely very sparse. The number of samples required for each additional dimension increases exponentially. The problem of sparse samples in space is called a dimensional disaster. Dimensionality reduction can alleviate this problem.

And why can we reduce the dimension, because the data is redundant, or some useless information or some repeated information, such as a 512 * 512 map only has a non-zero value in the center 100 * 100 area The remaining area is useless information, or a picture is center-symmetrical, then the symmetrical part of the information is repeated. The correct dimensionality of the data generally retains most of the important information of the original data, it can completely replace the input to do some other work, which can greatly reduce the amount of calculation. For example, drop to 2D or 3D to visualize.

From what point of view to reduce the dimensionality
Generally speaking, data dimensionality reduction can be considered from two angles. One is to directly extract feature subsets for feature extraction, for example, only the central part is taken from the 512*512 image, and the other is to adopt a linear/nonlinear method. It turns out that the high-dimensional space is transformed into a new space. The latter is mainly discussed here. The latter angle generally has two ideas to achieve, one is based on the mapping method from high regularized space to small regularized space this can be possible and

algorithm is PCA, and other LDA, Autoencoder is also considered.

The main purpose is to learn or calculate a matrix transformation W, which is multiplied by quality data to get unnecessary and unusual data. The other is a based learning method which uses manifolds. The purpose of manifold learning is to find low-dimensional descriptions of high-dimensional spatial samples. It assumes that the data will exhibit a regular method where quality that is low is placed on the above preference when compared but this the regular arrangement and cannot be directly measured by the Euclidean distance of the above plane that is present and monitored. As shown in the below, the actual distance between them on a whole should be described easily of the lower right necessity.

If there is a way to describe the manifold in high-dimensional space, then this spatial relationship can be preserved in the process of dimensionality reduction. This manifold category can be easily distinguished and monitored using various different techniques of high-dimensional space still has the property of European space. That is, their distance can be calculated by Esplanade, or a point coordinate can be calculated by a linear combination of adjacent nodes (LLE) so that a relationship of high-dimensional space can be obtained, and this relationship can be in low-dimensional space. It is retained to perform dimensionality reduction based on this relationship representation, so manifold learning can be used to compress data, visualize, obtain effective distance matrices, and so on.

Hyperparameter tuning

In deep neural networks, the adjustment of hyperparameters is an indispensable skill. By observing the monitoring indicators such as loss and accuracy in the training process, it is necessary to judge the training state of the current model and adjust the hyperparameters in time to be more scientific. The ground training model can improve resource utilization. The following hyperparameters were used in this study. The adjustment rules for different hyperparameters are introduced and summarized below.

(1) Learning rate

Learning rate is the basis of the machine learning terminology and can be clearly understood that this can help models increase their parametric structure. To further analyze it based on various consequences you need to give access to various other examples that are of no interest to the complexity. Different optimization algorithms determine different learning rates. When the learning probability increases the model may get an abrupt and the loss will continue to fluctuate up and down; if the learning rate is too small, the model can attain everything it needs slowly and can require longer training. Usually lr takes the value [0.01, 0.001, 0.0001]

(2) Batch size

This is basically the other technique that can be used and can be sent into the model. In a convolutional neural network, large batches usually make the network converge faster, but due to memory resource limitations, too large batches may result in insufficient memory. Or the program kernel crashes. Batch_size usually takes the value [16,32,64,128]

(3) Optimizer

Adam is currently an optimizer that converges quickly and is often used. Although the stochastic gradient descent (SGD) is slower, the momentum can accelerate the convergence, and the stochastic gradient descent algorithm with the momentum has a better optimal solution, that is, the model will have higher accuracy after convergence. Usually, if you are looking for speed, use Adam more.

(4) Number of iterations

Iterations also known as the number of possibilities that a model can use to attain the learning stage it aspires. We can use iterations to increase the hyperparameter tuning and also can use it to attain various other necessary elements such as the current iteration number is considered to be appropriate; when the test error rate becomes smaller and then becomes larger, the number of iterations is over. Larger, you need to reduce the number of iterations, otherwise, it will be easy to overfit.

(5) Activation function

In the neural network, the activation function does not really activate what but uses the activation function can be used to give some nonlinear and unnecessary restrictions so that the complexity of the model can be increased. For example, some problems are linearly separable, and more problems in real-world scenarios are not linearly separable. If you do not use the activation function, it is difficult to fit nonlinear problems, and the test will have low accuracy.

So, the activation function is mainly non-linear, such as sigmoid. The sigmoid function is usually used for two classifications, but to prevent the gradient from disappearing, it is suitable for shallow neural networks and needs to be equipped with smaller initialization weights. The than function has central symmetry and is suitable for categorization with symmetry. In deep learning, relu is the most used activation function, which avoids the disappearance of gradients.

Hyperparameters are some parameter values preset in machine learning before the start of algorithm training.

These parameter values cannot generally be changed by the algorithm itself, such as Manhattan distance and Euclidean distance in the KNN algorithm. The number of clusters N in the K-Means algorithm, the learning rate lr of deep learning; the opposite is the parameters that can be learned through training in the algorithm, such as weight w, offset b, and so on. The determination of the hyperparameters can be done by cross-validation.

Data sets can be divided into training sets, verification sets, and test sets.

1) The training set is a sample for learning, which is used to determine the coefficients in machine learning or deep learning, which generally account for 50%-60% or more of all samples;

2) The verification set is used to adjust the classifier parameters. In the sample set, during the training process, the network model will immediately verify the verification set. We will observe the performance of the verification set data on the model, whether the loss

function will decrease, and whether the accuracy rate is increasing. About 25-20% of the sample;

3) The ability of the test set to test the model (mainly classification ability), generally accounting for 20% or less.

Thus, by a clear explanation, we have learned about dimensionality reduction and hyperparameter tuning in detail. We will also learn about various machine learning algorithms in detail in the next chapter. This machine learning algorithms chapter will end the first section of our Machine learning and we will continue with deep learning in the next section.

Chapter 10: Machine Learning Algorithms

In Machine Learning, it can be divided into Supervised Learning, Unsupervised Learning, semi-Supervised Learning, and Reinforcement Learning according to different tasks.

Supervised Learning training data contains class information, such as in spam detection, its training samples contain class information: SPAM and non-spam. In supervised learning, the typical problems are Classification and Regression, and the typical algorithms are Logistic Regression, BP neural network, and linear Regression.

Unlike supervised learning, the training data for Unsupervised Learning contain no classified information. In unsupervised learning, the typical problem is clustering, which means K-Means Algorithm, DBSCAN Algorithm and so on.

Part of Semi-Supervised Learning training data contains category information, and part of data does not contain category information, which is the combination of supervised Learning and Unsupervised Learning. In the third type of algorithm, the algorithm is usually extended to the supervised learning algorithm to model unlabeled data.

About supervised learning algorithms in detail

The concept of Supervised Learning is briefly introduced in the front. Supervised Learning is an important Learning method in Machine Learning algorithm. In Supervised Learning, the training samples contain both feature and label information. Classification and Regression are the two most important algorithms in supervised learning. The main difference between them is that the tags in the Classification algorithm are discrete values, such as { + 1,- 1} in the Ad Click problem The label values in the regression algorithm are continuous value s. For example, the age of a person can be predicted by information such as a person's height, sex, and weight.

How does it work?

For a specific supervised learning task, the first step is to get samples with attribute values, assuming m training samples {(Z (5) , U(3) , (v (8) , w(1)) , ... , (m (0) , r(d))} , and then preprocess the samples to filter the impurities in the data Retention of useful information is a process called f feature processing or feature extraction.

A supervised learning algorithm is used to obtain the hypothesis function from one region to another sample set. Supervised learning is the process s of learning the hypothesis function from the sample data and using it to predict the new data.

About Unsupervised Learning Algorithms in detail

Unsupervised Learning is another machine learning algorithm. Unlike supervised Learning, in Unsupervised Learning, the samples contain only features and no label information. Unlike Supervised Learning, which does not contain label information, it is not known at the time of Learning whether the classification results are correct.

How does it work?

For a specific unsupervised learning task, the first step is to obtain samples with EIGENVALUES. Suppose M training data { W (0) , W(1) , ... , W (infinite)} are used to process the m samples, and useful information is obtained This process is called feature processing or feature extraction. Finally, the samples are processed by the unsupervised learning algorithm, such as a clustering algorithm.

Clustering Algorithm is one of the most typical unsupervised learning algorithms. The clustering algorithm makes use of the features of the samples and divides the samples with similar features into the same category, regardless of what the category is.

In the clustering problem, the samples are clustered by comparing feature 1(whether they have wings) and feature 2(whether they have f ins). as observed from our results as described above sample 1 and sample 2 are more similar, and sample 3 and sample 4 are more similar, so sample 1 and sample 2 can be grouped into the same category Divide sample 3 and sample 4 into another category, regardless of what category sample 1 and sample 2 belong to.

In addition to the clustering algorithm, in unsupervised learning, another important algorithm is a dimension reduction. Dimensionally reduction which is one of the most challenging machine learning tasks can be used to analyze the difference between the dimensionality and logical intervention that the learning sample possesses.

Now we will discuss a few machine learning algorithms in detail in the next section.

1) Logistic Regression

Logistic Regression as always known as one of the most advanced classification algorithms that train positive and negative samples in the data to learn the sample characteristics and the hypothetical functions between sample labels. The Logistic Regression algorithm is typically Linear classifier Due to its low complexity and easy implementation, the algorithm has been widely used in industry, such as: Using Logistic Regression Algorithm to achieve ad click-through rate prediction.

For a classification problem, usually can be divided into linear separable and linear inseparable two kinds. A classification problem is said to be linearly separable if it can be correctly classified using a linear discriminant function.

For the Logistic Regression algorithm, the parameters in the splitter hyperplane that need to be solved are the weight matrix that defines the weight and the complex interventions they possess when combined with various sources. By using which methods these irregular functions can be changed? Loss function also plays a major role in defining the result.

Loss function

In Logistic Regression Algorithm, the negative Log-likelihood function is usually used as its loss function, that is, the negative Log-likelihood (NLL) is used as its loss function What needs to be calculated is the minimum value of the NLL.

Implement Logistic regression using python:

With this theoretical preparation in mind, we then build a Logistic Regression classifier using the functions we have completed. We use the Linear separability data () as a training sample to make things easy when we are doing machine learning complex applications. In the process of building the model, there are two main steps: 1 training the model using the training sample; 2 New samples can be determined using various algorithms that are not necessary or useful.

First, we use the training samples to train the model. To enable Python to support Chinese annotations and use numpy tools, we need to add the following

Code:

```
# coding: UTF-8
import numpy as np
```

In the main function of listing , the main steps of training LR model include: 1 Import Training Data, as shown in the program code, as shown in 1, import training data load function as shown in Listing ; 2 use gradient descent to train the training data to get the model of the Logistic Regression algorithm, that is, the weight in the model, as shown in 2 in the Program Code; 3 output the weight in the file weights, as shown in 3 in the program code The save function to save the final model is shown in listing .

Python code is here:

```
print(" ............. Give data ............")
feature,label- givedata( "input.txt")
# 2nd point
print(" ..............Training............")
w= train( feature,500,0.02)
# 3rd step
print(" ...........Model saved.........")
output("weights,"  "w")
```

In the next program code, we will get a more detailed implementation of load function of the training data.

Python code is here:

```python
def data(filename) :
input : name(strng)
output: feature(tel)
f = open (filename)
feature = []
label = []
for read()
  featuretemporary = []
  labletemporary = []
  feature.append()

f.close()
return
```

In the load function, its input is the training data location, its output is the training data characteristic and the training data weight.

Forecasting new data:

For the classification algorithm, the trained model needs to be able to partition the new data set. Using the above steps, we train the LR model and save it in the "weights" file, at which point we need to use the trained LR model to predict the new data In order to be able to use the functions in numpy and support for Chinese annotations, at the beginning of the file "LR.

Python code here:

```
if_name = main
#1ststep
print (."  ........ model............")
w= loadweigh(w)
n = op.shape();
print(."  .......... load data.........")
test = load()
print(."  ........predict............")
h = predict(testdata)
```

In the prediction of the new Dataset, the first is to import the parameter s of the trained model, as shown in 1, and the function load of the imported model as shown in the listing. Second, you need to import test data, as shown in program 2, the test data import function load as shown in the listing. After both the model and the test data are imported, the model is used to predict the new data, as shown in 3 in the program, and the function predicate is implemented as shown in listing. Finally, you need to save the prediction to a file, as shown in 4 in the Program Code, and the implementation of the save function is shown in the listing.

Python code here:

```
f = open(w)
for f.readlines()
w_tmp = []
f.close()
```

you first need to import the numpy module and the SIG function in Lr. In the load function, the input is where the weight is, and in the import function, its value is imported into the weight matrix.

In the load function of the imported test set, the input is the number of positions and features of the test set, the number of features used to determine whether the test set meets the requirements, as shown in the code in 1 if it does not meet the requirements, it is discarded.

In the prediction function, the input is the feature of the test data and the weight of the model, and the output is the final prediction. The final prediction result is obtained by the product of feature and weight, and then the Sigmoid function is obtained. Here, the SIG function is used in the file "LR, " so in the file "Lr, " you need to import the SIG function:

import sig

When calculating the final output, in order to convert the probability value of the Sigmoid function output to {0,1} , it is usually possible to take 0. 5 as the boundary.

np.shape(result)
result.close()

The function save implementation saves the prediction to a specified file, saves the file name file and the predicted result as input to the function save, and finally writes the data in result to the file.

2) Softmax Regression Algorithms

Because of the low complexity and easy implementation of Logistic Regression Algorithm, it is widely used in the industry, such as calculating the click-through rate prediction in advertisements. However, the Logistic Regression algorithm is mainly used to deal with binary classification problems, if you need to deal with multi-classification problems, such as handwriting recognition, that is, the recognition of numbers in $\{0,1, \dots , 9\}$, then you need to use an algorithm that can deal with multi-classification problems.

The Softmax Regression algorithm is an extension of the Logistic Regression algorithm for multiclass classification problems, where any two classes are linear separability

Multiple classification problems:

The Logistic Regression Algorithm introduced in the previous chapter is mainly used to deal with binary classification problems. The number of Class Label Y is 2, that is, y ∈{0,1} or y ∈{-1,1} . There is, however, a problem with multiple classifications, where the number of values for class label Y is greater than 2, such as handwritten character recognition, where the recognition is a number in {0,1, ... , 9} .

handwriting is selected from the MNIST Dataset. In the MNIS T handwritten character recognition Dataset, the handwritten characters need to be divided into 10 categories of 0 ~ 9. In general, such multi-classification problems can be partitioned using multiple binary classification algorithms. Similarly, there are some algorithms dedicated to multi-classification problems, such as the SoftMax Regression algorithm.

The gradient update function gradient Ascent is the core program of the SoftMax Regression algorithm, implementing the update of the weights in the SoftMax Regression model. The input to the gradient ascent is sent to the total number of required classes with a variable dataset with a number of iterations and rounded circles that we need to learn and the learning step alpha in the gradient descent. The output of the function is the model weight of the SoftMax Regression. The function cost calculates the value of the loss function, as shown in the program code, and the cost function is implemented. Using the gradient descent, the weight in the model is updated based on the calculated error.

Predictions for new data:

For the classification algorithm, the trained model needs to be able to partition the new data set. Using the above steps, we train the SOFTMAX Regression model and store it in the "weights" file. At this point, we need to use the trained Max Regression model to predict the new data In order to be able to use functions in numpy and support for Chinese annotations, start with the file "SOFTMAX" , we're in:

```
results = predict(test_data)
test_dat = load_data(3000,0.3)
saveresult()
```

start by importing the model's parameters, as shown in 1 in the program code, and implement the load function as shown. A t the same time, you need to import the test data, as shown in the program Code 2, the load function as shown in listing 2-8. Then use the training of SoftMax model to predict the test data, as shown in the program code in 3, the predict function as shown in the listing. The final prediction is saved to a file result, as shown in 4 in the program code, and the save function is implemented d as shown in the listing.

```
w_tmp = []
lines = line.strip()
w.append()
f.close()
```

You need to import the random module; whose main function is to generate the following test data. In the load function, its input is the model weight file weights, and its output is the weight Matrix, as well as the weight Matrix's row number M and column number N.

The load function is used to generate a test sample, where the input of the function is the number of samples, Num, and the dimension of the samples, M. The output is the generated test sample testDataSet. The random () method in the random module, which is used in sample generation, is primarily to generate random numbers between (0.0,1.0). Therefore, you need to import the random module in the `SOFTMAXx" file:

import random as rd

Generate a prediction:
The predict function predicts the test data and stores the final prediction to H, and the predicate function is entered as the weight weights for the test data and the model the output of the function is the category for each test sample. In Function 1, the probability of each sample belonging to each category is obtained, and finally, the index with the highest probability value is returned at 2 as the final category label.

for i in xrange[m]

f.write()

f.close()

The function save saves the final prediction result to the specified file. The input to the save function is the final prediction result and the saved file name, file, respectively.

3) Support Vector Machine

Support vector machine is one of the famous algorithms that need to be understood before trying to obtain the effectiveness of it. Get ready to use it for different purposes. Support Vector Machine has been paid more and more effectiveness in the technological and research field due to its advantages in various fields and has been widely used in a short time. The Support vector machine is recognized as an excellent classification model, and the theoretical research of the Support vector machine has been developed synchronously Support Vector machine provides strong theoretical support for the study.

In perceptron algorithms, the final separating hyperplane is obtained by minimizing the distance between misclassified samples and the separating hyperplane, but for Perceptron Algorithms, the initial value of separating hyperplane parameters W and B and the order of selecting misclassified samples have influence on the calculation of the final separating hyperplane, using different initial values or different misclassified points the final separation hyperplane is different.

In general, the distance of a sample point from the separating hyperplane can indicate the degree of confidence in classification prediction. Sample point a is farthest from the hyperplane, and if it is predicted to be positive, then we are more confident that the prediction is correct. To indicate the degree of confidence in the classification prediction, Functional Margin, and Geometric Margin are defined respectively.

In the Perceptron Algorithm, we note that the distance of sample point x (I) from the separating hyperplane can be represented relatively if the separating hyperplane W X + B is determined. When the predicted value W X (I) + B is the same as the sample label y (I), it indicates that the final classification is correct. Therefore, Y (I)(W X (I) + B) can be used to indicate the correctness and reliability of the classification, which is the definition of the function interval.

The function interval can indicate the correctness and certainty of classification prediction. However, in the separated hyperplane, if the parameters W and B are doubled at the same time, there is no change in the separated hyperplane, but in the case of the function interval, it is doubled. To solve this problem, we introduce geometric spacing.

SMO algorithm

By means of Joseph-Louis Lagrange's duality, we transform the original constrained optimization this duality problem into the problem of normal model optimization. This can further be enhanced in different options. Finally, we get the solution to the options that constantly support Weight and Variance. For the constrained optimization problem above, how should we solve it?

For the above-constrained problem that has no optimizations programming that is without any restrictions are used. During the development of Svm, many can be used to define the rare consequential system that can be understood efficiently in 1998, Sequential Minimal Optimization (SMO) algorithm proposed by Platt was widely used.

Build SVM using python:

Next, we build a complete SVM classifier using Python. In the process of constructing SVM classifier, the training of SVM classifier and the classification of unknown data by Svm classifier are included. In practice, we first create a "svm.py " file. The "SVM.py " document contains SVM model training and SVM model used to predict the function of unknown data.

In the training process of the SVM model, the main documents used include "SVM.py " and "SVM." First, we declare a class for the SVM model and open the "Url" file. To make the Python file support Chinese annotations and related calculations for using matrices in the SVM, we need to add at the beginning of the " SVM.py " file:

import numpy as np

At the same time, after training the SVM classifier, we need to save the S VM model to local, at this time, we need to use the CPICKLE module, and we need to import the module:

import cPickle as input

Python code is given here:
self.train = dataset
self.kernal_opt = kernel_option;
self.kernel_mat = kernel_maths;

The class of the SVM model is implemented. In the class of the SVM model, the training data of SVM model and the parameters of the SVM model are included. The CALC function is used to compute the kernel matrix of the sample based on the specified kernel, as shown in 1 of the Program Code. The CALC function is implemented as shown.

cal_kernel_value (self.kernal_x ,train_x)

Ki, J represents the value of the kernel function between the I sample and the J sample. During the calculation, the value of the kernel function between each sample and other sample is calculated by using the CAL function, as shown in 1 in the Program Code The actual implementation of the function call is shown in the listing.

the CAL function is used to compute the value of the kernel function between the sample train and all other samples based on the specified kernel type and the parameter kernel calculation. In the process of implementation, only the GAUSS kernel is implemented, as shown in the program Code 1, Gauss Kernel in the specific form as shown in section. If no kernel type is specified, the kernel is not used by default, as shown in 2 in the program code.

bound_samples = []

return svm

The function SVM selects the first I to be optimized by alternately traversing the non-boundary samples or all samples, giving preference to traversing the non-boundary samples because the non-boundary samples are more likely to need an adjustment the boundary samples are often left on the boundary without further adjustment. The non-boundary samples are iterated and the non-boundary samples which violate the KKT condition are selected to adjust until all the non-boundary samples satisfy the KKT condition.

When a traversal finds that no non-bounded samples are adjusted, all samples are traversed to verify that the entire set satisfies the KKT condition. If some samples are further optimized in the test of the whole set, it is necessary to iterate over the non-boundary samples. In this way, we keep switching between "traversing all samples" and "traversing non-boundary samples" until the whole training set satisfies the KKT condition. After selecting the first variable I, you need to determine if it satisfies the condition, and you need to select the second variable j, as shown in the program code in 1 and 2, and the realization of the function choose is shown in the listing.

```
svm.alphas
update_error[tmp]
if ( 0 > svm.alphas)
return null
else
 return 0
```

The function selected is used to select the second variable, j. for the second variable, the selection criterion is that the error value changes the most, as shown in 1 in the program code. If at this point, the length of the candidate set is 0, J is selected at random, as shown in 2 in the Program Code.

The function call uses a trained SVM model to predict the training sample, as shown in 1 in the Program Code; after the predicted values are obtained, they are compared with their labels If the symbol of the predicted value is consistent with the symbol of the real value, then the prediction is accurate, otherwise the prediction is not accurate, the comparison process is as shown in 2 in the Program Code.

```
predict(float)
predict = kernal_value.T
np.multiply
return predict
```

Training of the SVM model is :

```
Iteration: 0
Iteration: 1
Iteration: 3
```

Save the model

For the classification algorithm, the trained model needs to be able to partition the new data set. Using the above steps, we train the Support vector machine SVM model and save it in the "model" file. At this time, we need to use the trained SVM model to predict the new data In order to be able to use the functions in numpy and support for Chinese annotations, start with the file "SVM"

import numpy as SVM

At the same time, in the process of forecasting new data, we need to use the CPICKLE module for Model Import, we need to use the SVM function in the "svm.py " file, therefore, we need to import these modules in the `SVMm" file:

import cPickel as pickel
from svm import svm_predict

Thus, we end our discussion about the support of a vector machine in detail.

4) Random forests

For a complex classification problem, training a complex classification model is usually time-consuming. This can be used to determine the prediction capability of random forests with a lot of precision. we can usually choose to train multiple classification models the final prediction can be obtained by combining the results of each prediction. Ensemble Learning is such a Learning method, Ensemble Learning refers to a variety of learning algorithms, through the appropriate form of combination to complete the same task. In ensemble learning, there are bagging algorithm and a boosting algorithm.

Basics about decision tree

In the classification problem, Decision Tree Algorithm divides samples into different categories by the value of one-dimension attribute. In the case of the binary classification, the data set for the binary classification.

There are 5 samples, the attributes of the samples are "whether to breathe with Gills" and "with or without fins." By learning from the samples, such as "Whale

Shark," we can use the learned decision tree model for a new sample to make a correct decision is to judge whether it is a fish or not.

the function cal is used to calculate the Gini index of the data set. In calculating the Gini Index, the number of category labels in the data set is determined, and the label function is used to calculate the number of different category labels in the data set as shown in 1 in the Program Code, the function label is implemented as shown in the listing. By counting the number of different categories of labels, and according to the above calculation method, we calculate the Gini index in the current data set data, the concrete calculation method is as shown in the program Code 2 and 3, in the calculation of Gini Index, you need a POW function, so before we start, WE NEED TO IMPORT POW:

from math import pow

This is a special type of application of decision tree and can be used in various different purposes. As mentioned above, the main decision Tree models are the ID3 algorithm, C4.5 algorithm and CART algorithm Cart can deal with both classification and regression problems.

Construction of the classification tree

In CART classification tree algorithm, the Gini index is used as the index of dividing the number, and the samples are divided by the features of the samples until all the samples in the leaf nodes are of the same class The CART classification tree construction process looks like this:

* For the current training Dataset, traversing all attributes and their possible shard points to find the best shard attributes and their best shard points to minimize the Keeny index after Shard Using this optimal attribute and its optimal cut point, the training data set is divided into two subsets, the result of which is the left subtree and the result is the right subtree.

* Repeat the following steps until the Stop Condition is met: find the best split attribute and its best split point for each leaf node, and divide it into left and right subtrees.

* generating a CART decision tree

Python code here:

```
class node

self.results = result
self.right = right
self.left = left
```

The node class is set for the node in the tree. In the node class, the attribute FEA represents the index value of the feature to be sliced, and the attribute value represents the specific value at the index of the feature to be sliced when the node is a leaf node The attribute results represents the category of the leaf node, the attribute right represents the right subtree of the node in the tree, and the attribute left represents the left subtree of the node in the tree.

```
if boostgain>0
buildtree
else
return null;
```

The function build is used to construct a CART classification tree. In the process of constructing a CART classification tree, the main steps are as follows: 1 calculating the current Gini Index; 2 trying to divide the tree into left and right subtrees according to each feature in the data set Calculate the best partition, continue to divide the left and right subtrees by iteration; 3 judges whether the Division can continue at present, it cannot continue to divide, quit.

In the division process, need to follow the Gini Index to find the best division. To find the best method of partition is to traverse all the sample feature s, and get the feature which can make the biggest change of Gini index before and after partition, divide the tree into left and right subtrees according to the value of the feature. In the search for the best partition, first, take all possible values of the sample at the FEA feature and store them in the dictionary feature, as shown in 2 of the Program Code. For each possible value at the characteristic FEA, use the function split to try to divide the data set into left and right subtrees set and set, as shown in 3 in the Program

Code. The function split splits the data set into left and right subtrees according to the value at the specified characteristic. The implementation of the function split is shown in listing. After dividing, calculate the Gini Index at this time, the Gini Index is the sum of the Gini Index of the left and right subtrees, as shown in code 4. Judge the current Gini Index and the change of the Gini Index before the partition, and find the feature which can make the biggest change of the Gini index like the final partition standard, as shown in 5 of the Program Code.

Python code is here:

```
set_1 =[]
set_2 = []
for y in data
if (x >2)
append
else ;
set.append
quit
```

The function split is primarily used to split a feature when its value is a continuous value. When the value at the feature FEA is a continuous value, and when the value at that location is greater than or equal to the value to be split, the sample is split into sets as shown in 1 in the Program Code, otherwise, it is divided into sets, as shown in 2 in the Program Code.

Chapter 11: Introduction to Neural Networks

This part of the book deals with deep learning and neural networks in detail. We will first learn about Recommender systems and deep learning in detail before going to start about a python implementation of an artificial neural network in detail.

In machine learning algorithms, there are other classification methods besides supervised learning and unsupervised learning according to the classification mentioned above, such as the function of the Algorithm is divided into classification algorithm, regression algorithm, clustering Algorithm and Dimension Reduction Algorithm. With the continuous development of machine learning, there are many new research directions, recommendation algorithm and deep learning is more research directions in recent years.

About the Recommendation system

Because of the huge availability of information from different sources the data may sometimes reach its peak limit. When the users have no definite information demand, they cannot get the information of interest from a large amount of information the rapid increase in the amount of information has also led to a large amount of information buried, unable to reach some potential users. The advent of Recommendation System (RS) is called the bridge between users and information. This is basically necessary because it will help people to choose their data from a bunch of data and at the same time, it can pass valuable information to the potential users.

In the recommendation system, recommendation algorithms play an important role, commonly used recommendation Algorithms are: one is of filtering algorithm known as collaborative filtering whereas other one deals with Matrix decomposition and the final one is recommendation Algorithm based on the graph.

Deep Learning

Traditional machine learning algorithms use shallow-layer structures, which generally contain at most one or two layers of nonlinear feature transformation. Shallow-layer structures are more effective in solving many simple problems but there are many problems when dealing with more complex and natural signals.

As computers evolved, people tried to use deep structures to deal with these more complex problems, but they also encountered a lot of difficulties until 2006, when Hinton and others came up with the concept of layer by layer training Deep learning has once again entered people's field of vision, the increasing amount of data and the enhancement of computer computing power, making deep learning technology possible. In deep learning, several common models include 1 Self encoder model, which constructs deep network by Stack Self Encoder; 2 convolutional Neural Network Model, which constructs deep network by convolution layer and sampling layer; 3 recurrent neural networks.

Now in this section, we will start knowing about neural networks in detail. Neural Networks surprisingly are there in the tech phenomenon from more than fifty years but didn't get much recognition or funding due to the fact that there are no good hardware and graphical resources. But in the past decade due to the significant increase in the gaming industry, we now have access to graphical processors that can handle the neural networks of different types. In this section, we will give a brief description of the neural networks along with its implementation.

Neurons:

Neurons are the most pivotal part of neural networks. The basic principle on how they work is by taking an input (whatever it may be) and apply mathematics to the input in a conditional that we would get an output.

Neural networks in detail:

The most popular technology at the moment is definitely artificial intelligence. The underlying model of artificial intelligence is the neural network. Many complex applications (such as pattern recognition, automatic control) and advanced models (such as deep learning) are based on it. Learning artificial intelligence must start with it.

First, the sensor

Historically, scientists have always wanted to simulate the human brain and create machines that can be thought of. Why can people think? Scientists have discovered that the reason lies in the neural network of the human body.

- External stimuli are transformed into electrical signals through nerve endings and transduced into nerve cells (also called neurons).
- Numerous neurons form the nerve center.
- The nerve center synthesizes various signals and makes judgments.
- The human body responds to external stimuli according to instructions from the nerve center.

Since the basis of thinking is neurons, if you can "artificial neuron," you can form an artificial neural network to simulate thinking. In the 1960s, the earliest "artificial neuron" model, called perceptron, was still in use today.

The circle above shows a perceptron. It accepts multiple inputs (x1, x2, x3...) and produces an output, like the nerve endings that sense changes in various external environments, and finally produce electrical signals.

To simplify the model, we have agreed that there are only two possibilities for each input: 1 or 0. If all inputs are 1, indicating that the various conditions are true, the output is 1; if all inputs are 0, the condition is not true and the output is 0.

Second, the example of the sensor

Let's look at an example. The city is holding an annual game animation exhibition, Xiao Ming cannot decide, whether to visit on weekends.

He decided to consider three factors.

- Weather: Is it sunny on weekends?
- Companion: Can you find someone to go with?
- Price: Is the ticket affordable?

This constitutes a perceptron. The above three factors are external inputs, and the final decision is the output of the sensor. If all three factors are Yes (indicated by 1), the output is 1 (to visit); if they are all No (using 0), the output is 0 (do not visit).

Third, the weight and threshold

Seeing this, you will definitely ask: If some factors are true, other factors are not established, what is the output? For example, the weekend is good weather, tickets are not expensive, but cannot find a companion, he still wants to visit?

In reality, various factors are rarely equally important: some factors are decisive factors, and others are secondary factors. Therefore, you can assign weights to these factors, representing their different importance.

- Weather: weight is 8
- Companion: weight is 4
- Price: weight 4

The above weights indicate that weather is a decisive factor, and both peers and prices are secondary factors.

If all three factors are 1, the sum of their multiplied by the weight is 8 + 4 + 4 = 16. If the weather and price factors are 1, and the companion factor is 0, the sum becomes 8 + 0 + 4 = 12.

At this time, you also need to specify a threshold. If the sum is greater than the threshold, the sensor outputs 1 and otherwise outputs 0. Assuming a threshold of 8, then 12 > 8, raja decided to visit. The level of the threshold represents a strong will and the lower the threshold, the more you want to go, the higher you want to go.

The above decision process uses mathematical expressions as follows.

In the above formula, x represents various external factors, and w represents the corresponding weight.

Fourth, the decision model

A single perceptron constitutes a simple decision model that can be used. In the real world, the actual decision model is much more complicated, and it is a multi-layer network composed of multiple perceptron's.

The underlying sensor receives the external input, and after making a judgment, sends a signal as the input of the upper sensor until the final result is obtained. (Note: The output of the Sensor is still only one, but can be sent to multiple targets.)

The signals are unidirectional. In reality, there may be a cyclical transmission, that is, A is passed to B, B is passed to C, and C is passed to A. This is called recurrent neural network.

Fifth, vectorization

In order to facilitate the discussion that follows, some mathematical processing is required on the above model.

- The external factors x1, x2, x3 are written as vectors <x1, x2, x3>, abbreviated as x
- The weights w1, w2, and w3 are also written as vectors (w1, w2, w3), abbreviated as w
- Define the operation $w \cdot x = \sum wx$, the point operation of w and x, equal to the sum of the product of the factor and the weight
- Define b equal to the negative threshold b = - threshold

The perceptron model becomes the following.

Sixth, the operation process of the neural network

The building strategy of a neural network needs to meet three conditions.

- Input and output

- Weight (w) and threshold (b)
- Multilayer perceptron structure

In other words, you need to draw the picture that appears above.

Among them, the most difficult part is to determine the weight (w) and the threshold (b). So far, these two values are subjectively given, but in reality, it is difficult to estimate their values, there must be a way to find out.

This method is a trial and error method. The other parameters are unchanged, and a small change in w (or b) is recorded as Δw (or Δb), and then the output is observed to change. Repeat this process until the set of w and b corresponding to the most accurate output is the value we want. This process is called training of the model.

Therefore, the operation of the neural network is as follows.
- Determine input and output
- Find one or more algorithms that can get output from the input
- Find a set of data for known answers to train the model and estimate w and b

- Once the new data is generated, enter the model and you will get the results and correct the w and b.

As you can see, the whole process requires massive calculations. Therefore, neural networks have only been of practical value in recent years, and the general CPU is not working. It is calculated using a GPU specifically designed for machine learning.

Seven, an example of a neural network

The neural network is explained below by an example of automatic license plate recognition.

The so-called "automatic license plate recognition" means that the probe of the highway takes a photo of the license plate, and the computer recognizes the number in the photo.

In this example, the license plate photo is the input, the license plate number is the output, and the sharpness of the photo can be set to weight (w). Then, find one or more image comparison algorithms as perceptron' s. The result of the algorithm is a probability, for example, the probability of 75% can be determined to be the number 1. This requires setting a threshold (b) (such as 85% confidence) below which the result is invalid.

A set of recognized license plate photos, as a training set data, input model. Constantly adjust various parameters until you find the combination of parameters with the highest correct rate. If you get a new photo later, you can give the result directly.

Eight, the continuity of the output

There is a problem with the above model that has not been resolved. According to the assumption, the output has only two results: 0 and 1. However, the model requires a small change in w or b, which will cause a change in the output. If only 0 and 1 are output, it is too insensitive, and the correctness of the training cannot be guaranteed. Therefore, the "output" must be transformed into a continuity function.

This requires a simple mathematical transformation.
First, the calculation result wx + b of the perceptron are denoted as z.

z = wx + b

Then, calculate the following equation and record the result as σ(z).

$$\sigma(z) = 1 / (1 + e^{\wedge}(-z))$$

This is because if z tends to positive infinity z → +∞ (indicating that the perceptron strongly matches), then σ(z) → 1; if z tends to negative infinity z → -∞ (indicating that the perceptron strongly does not match), then σ(z) → 0. That is, as long as σ(z) is used as the output, the output becomes a continuity function.

The original output curve is as follows.

This chapter just gave a basic overview of the neural networks and its importance. In the next chapter, we will use artificial neural networks with python to create various use cases.

Chapter 12: Advanced Understanding of Neural Networks

In this chapter, we will discuss in detail about the artificial neural network along with its implementation in python. We will dive in details in the next two chapters to get a good understanding of the topic. Let us start.

What are Artificial Neural Networks?

Artificial Neural Network (Ann) which basically is inspired from the structure of the human brain, is an intelligent system that imitates the information processing function of the human brain's Neural system Artificial intelligence (AI) has been a research hotspot since the 1980s. In different stages of neural network development, different neural network models have emerged, from the initial shallow neural network to the deep neural network now in full swing.

In the development of neural network technology, the emergence and development of BP (Back Propagation) are one of the famous algorithms in the development of the whole neural network diaspora. This particular neural network usually refers to a shallow neural network with a three-layer network structure.

The activation functions of neural networks:

The interval for the Sigmoid function is [0,1], and the interval for the Tanh function is [-1,1]. If you use sigmoid as the starting point that is activation function then the result is 1, the Neuron is activated, otherwise, it is not activated. Similarly, when the activation function is Tanh and the output of the Neuron is 1, the Neuron is activated or not.

Neural network model:

A neural network basically is a replica of a bunch of neurons in the central nervous system. In a neural network, input and output are mutually relatable, and the + 1 term represents the offset term. A neural network that is basically divided into three layers by precision, in which layer $l1$ represents the input part whereas layer $l2$ is covered as a hidden layer and out of all these layer L3 is called as output layer.

In a neural network, there are several main parameters:

* Layers of the network nl. The number of layers NL 3 in the neural network shown. For the neural network described above, the input layer is I1 and the output layer is L3.

* Network weights and offsets (W, B)(W (7) , B (5) , W (9) , B (6)) , which represent the connection parameters between the J neuron at level I and the I neuron at level L + 1, labeled is the bias term for the I neuron at level L + 1. In the neural network , W (1) $\in$ R 33, W (2)$\in$ R 13.

Computation of neural networks:

In a neural network, the input and output are mutually related. Let 's say that we're talking about the input of the I neuron, let's say that we mainly concentrate on the neuron that is of output, where, when I 1, According to the parameters such as bias of the above neural network, we can calculate different characteristics such as output of this particular network and then move forward to learn about the final output that represents many things. These steps are called forward propagation and refer to the propagation of a signal from one side of a neuron that is input to another side that is output to be precise.

Loss function:

The idea is this: for a given set of training data (X, Y) , a forward propagation algorithm calculates the output value of each neuron, and when the output of all the neurons has been calculated, the Backpropagation Calculate "residuals" for each neuron, such as the residuals of layer I neuron I can be expressed as. The residuals represent the effect of the Neuron on the final residuals. There are two main cases: one is that the neuron is an output neuron, the other is that the neuron is a non-output Neuron. Suppose that the weighted sum of the inputs of the I neuron at level L is represented, and the output of the I neuron at level L is represented.

Learning process of Neural Network:

For the advanced implementation of neural networks, there are several steps:

1) Initialization parameters, including weight, bias, network layer structure, activation functions, and so on.

2) Circular computation

3) Forward propagation, computational error

4) Back-propagation, adjusting parameters

5) Return to the final neural network model

Python implementation:

Now, let's use Python to implement the above update process for the BP neural network. The first step we need to do is to import functions by using different strategies.

import numpy as np
from math import functionname

Here functionname is sqrt (square root)

The function BP implements the training of the network, whose input is the feature of the data that is prepared , the usage of the training data is the number of present Nodes that are invisible , and the peak number of revolutions maxCycle . The learning rate Alpha during gradient descent and the number of final nodes that are outside represented by N.

The output is a model of Backpropagation neural network, including a layer that is not present to that is hidden by the weight of the source w 0 and Bias B 0, from invisible to farthest layer weight w 1 and bias B 1. Prior to model training, the weights W0 and biasing B0 from the easiest layer to access to the invisible layer, W1 and Biasing B1 from the invisible layer to the farthest layer present, are initialized as shown in 1,2,3, and 4 of the Program Code Generates a random number from the specified interval.

Python code:

```python
def bp_network(feature,label,alpha)
input : feature(mat)
output: w0(mat)
# 2nd step
while <= maxcycle
output_out = predict_out
delta_output = np.multiply
i +- 1
return w0,w1,b1,b2
```

Where a special characteristic function represents the sum of middle layer nodes, and another characteristic function is the number of somewhat nearer layer nodes. After the initialization of the neural network that is available is completed, the backpropagation neural network model is trained by using the already prepared and preprocessed data. The training process includes the following aspects: 1 the forward propagation of the signal, as shown by 5 in the Program Code; 2 the backpropagation of the error, as shown in 6 of the Program Code; 3 the parameters in the Backpropagation neural network that are in conveyance with the layer I are corrected by the error of backpropagation, as shown in 7 of the Program Code; 4 The value of the current loss function is calculated after every 100 generations As shown in 8 in the Program Code.

In the forward propagation of the signal, the BP neural network is divided into 1 calculating the hidden input, such as the hidden function in the Program Code, as shown in listing ; 2 calculating the hidden output, as the Program Code Hidden Function, hidden function as shown in Listing ; 3 to calculate the output layer of input, such as the program code, predict function, predict function as shown in listing 6-4; 4 this can be used to find the output of the output layer present, such as the code that is programmed and special functions like predicting function as shown in listing.

Python code:

```
def hidden_in(feature,wO,bO)
input: feature(mat)
output: hidden_in(mat)
```

```
m = np.shape(feature)
hidden_in = feature * wO
return hidden_in
```

The hidden function computes the hidden layer input. In Hidden, its input is the feature that trains the data, its input layer weight w 0 to the hidden layer and its input layer bias b 0 to the hidden layer, and its output is hidden due to the input function that is hidden. The method of calculation is described above.

```
input : hidden_in(mat)
output;hidden_out(mat)
```

The hidden function computes the hidden layer's output. Hidden in the function, its input is hidden, its output is hidden for the hidden layer's output. The calculation is to calculate the Sigmoid value for each value in hidden input, as shown in 1 in the Program Code, and the SIG function is implemented as shown.

```
def predict_in(hidden_out,w1,b1)
m = np.shape(hidden_out)
for i in range ( x>m)
return predict_n
```

The function predicts evaluates the input of the farthermost layer. In the function that needs to be predicted, the input that needs to be given is hidden from the invisible layer, the weight w 1 from the invisible layer to the farthest layer and the offset b 1 from the invisible layer to the farthest layer, and the characteristic result is predicted from the invisible layer that is present.

The function predicts evaluates the data came from the farthest layer. In the function that is needed to be predicted, the data given is the occurrence of the farthest layer, and the results that came is the farthest result of the output layer. This is done ne by calculating the Sigmoid value for each value in the input prediction of the output layer. Code is given below.

```
def sig(x)
input : x(mat/float)
```

output : sigmoid(mat/float)

return null

In the process of backpropagation concepts where we need to learn , the BP neural network is divided into 1 calculating the residual error that is from the invisible layer that is present to the farthest layer and 2 calculating the residual error that cannot be recreated from data given using layer to invisible layer. The partial function is used in the calculation of the residuals, and the partial function is implemented.

Code below:

```
def partial_sig(x)
input : x(mat/float)
output : cut(mat/float)
for i in range(x.m)
return out
```

When the weight of the BP neural network is updated, every 100 iterations, we need to calculate the value of the function that undergoes loss, get function is used to calculate the value of the loss that inhabits right then, get function as shown in the listing.

Code below:

```
def get_cost(cost)
input: cost(mat)
output : cost_sum / m (double)
m,n = np.shape(cost)

cost_sum = 0.0
for i in preferabledistance(input)
 for j in preferabledistance (output)
return cost/input
```

The input to the get function is the difference cost between the predicted value from the current BP neural network model and the sample label, and the output is the value of the current loss function.

In this complex manner, we can build neural networks. In the next chapter, we will deal in more detail about deep neural networks. Let us dive and get additional knowledge and implementation. This is a very complex topic so use your own interpretation to understand it better.

Chapter 13: Training Deep Neural Networks

In this chapter, we will dive into learning more about artificial deep neural network implementation in detail. This is by far the most complex chapter with weird code of TensorFlow. Just stay focused and use this information to understand how neural networks work.

There are many parameters in the BP neural network, some parameters cannot be selected through the gradient descent, and these parameters are called hyperparameters. In general, the optimal solution of the super parameter cannot be obtained. First of all, we cannot optimize each hyperparameter individually. Second, we can't use gradient descent directly because some super parameters are discrete and some are continuous. Finally, this is a nonconvex optimization problem, and finding a locally optimal solution takes a lot of effort. Over the years, researchers have devised a number of rules of thumb for selecting hyperparameters in a neural network. In addition to the selection of super-parameters, the selection of nonlinear transformation is also important in the BP neural network. Different nonlinear transformations have different properties.

Nonlinear Transformation

Nonlinear functions are always important and can help in different applications. Out of many nonlinear functions, sigmoid is considered a famous function that is used everybody followed by tanh function. Where the sigmoid function has an output mean of less than 0, this causes the next layer of neurons to receive a signal that is considered as an input. Unlike sigmoid functions, Tanh functions have an output mean of 0, so Tanh functions generally have better convergence.

Neural network algorithm practice:

In the process of using BP Neural Network Algorithm to classify them, there are two parts: 1 training the model with training data and 2 forecasting' s the new data.

Training BP neural network model mainly includes: 1 import training data, as shown in the program code, as shown in the load function of training data specific implementation that is shown vividly in the program code; 2 The Back propagations neural network model is prepared in nature by using the training data, as shown in 2 in the Program Code, the function of the trained data model in network that is of high importance is shown in listing in the program. 3 after the training, the trained BP model with high consistency is saved As visualized in 3 in the Program Code, the save function is implemented as shown in Listing ; 4 calculates the accuracy of the trained model with respect to the training data, at this point, we need to use the well prepared neural network model to estimate that needs to be used further, as shown in 4 in the program code, and then calculate the difference between the results that are strange and real deviating from fake results to get the perfection of trained model in training data set as shown in 5, the prediction function get is implemented as shown in listing, and the error rate function err is shown in listing.

Python code is here:

```
if_name = " main"
result = get_predict(feature,w0,w1,b0,b1)
```

```
err_rate(rp.argmax(label,axis))
np.argmax(result,axis)
```

Training BP neural network model mainly includes: 1 import training data, as shown in the program code, as shown in the load function of training data specific implementation as shown in the program Listing; 2 this network model that is present and important is fed with a lot of data and is used explicitly, as shown in 2 in the Program Code, the BP function of the trained BP model that is efficient is shown in listing in the program. 3 after the training, the trained BP model present in the process is explained as shown in the Program Code, the save function is implemented as shown in Listing; 4 calculates the accuracy of the trained model with respect to the training data, at this point, we need to use the well prepared and preprocessed model to predict the favorable data , as shown in 4 in the program code, and then calculate the difference between the results that are given and that will be given to get the accuracy of the model in the training data set As shown in 5, the prediction function get is implemented as shown in listing , and the error rate function err is shown in listing.

```
def thisdata(nameoffile)
x= open(nameoffile)
datapresent= []
presence_tmp = []
feature_tmp = []
feature_data.append()
f.close()
return exit;
```

The function load imports the training data into a feature array and a label array, respectively, into a feature array and a label array. In the process of getting the label, you need to count the number of categories in the training data As shown in 1 in the Program Code, for a label, such as {0,1} in the binary input label, during the conversion, you need to convert 0 to [1,0] and 1 to [0,1] , as shown in 2 in the Program Code.

```
def save_model(w0,w1,b0,b1)
def write-file(file_name,source):
f = open(file,"w")
f.close()
write.file('weightw0',wo)
write.file('weightw1',w1)
write.file('weightw2',w2)
write.file('weightw3',w3)
```

The function save saves the trained BP neural network model to its corresponding file. In the three-layer network structure, the parameters to be saved include the weight w 0 present between the layers that are said to be farthest and disappearing between layers that are subsequent and connected , weight W1 between disappearing layer and farthest layer , and Bias b1 between disappearing layer and farthest of the layer. The write function is defined in the save function to write the value in source to the file. The procedure to save w 0 is shown in 1, and the procedure to save w 1 is shown in 2 The procedure for saving B0 is shown in 3 of the Program Code, and the procedure for Saving B1 is shown in 4 of the Program Code.

The function err compares the result of the training, the pre, with the label in the sample, to calculate the error rate.

Python code here:
```
def err_rate(label,pre) :
input : label (mat)
pre (mat)
output : rate (float)
m = np.shape(label) [0]
return rate
```
Using the already prepared neural network with certain characteristics to estimate the new data, the main steps are: 1 import the new data set, as shown in the Program Code, import the load function of the new Dataset as shown in Listing ; 2 import the pre-prepared network model that is, import the concise parameters that are making up the model, as shown in Listing 2, the load function that is observed by network model is shown in

listing after both the BP neural network model and the test data are imported, the Model that is used in the process of the code is used to estimate the concentration of the data. The concrete implementation of the function get is shown in Listing of the program; 4 finally saves the predicted result to a specified file, as shown in listing 4 of the Program Code, and the concrete implementation of the save function, which saves the predicted result, as shown in the listing.

Python code here:

```
def load_data(file_name)
feature-data =[]
lines = line.strip()
feature-data.append()
f.close()
```

The load function imports the trained BP neural network model, which is stored in four files: File, file, file, and file. You need to import four files, as shown in 1,2,3, and 4 in the Program Code.

```
def save_predict
input : pre(mat)
f = open(file_name,"w")
result =[]
f.write("output')
f.close
```

The function save saves the predicted result, pre, to the file.

In this following manner, we implemented deep neural networks using python. This ends an advanced discussion about neural networks. In our next chapter, we will discuss the Recommendation algorithm which is a basic necessity and application of high data sets like webpages in detail.

Chapter 14: Scaling Neural Networks for Huge Datasets

This chapter deals with one of the most important technological advancements of machine learning and particularly about neural networks. We usually see recommendations on YouTube or Amazon or any other social networking website. This is basically done using neural network principles that made the world competent and beautiful. We will learn about their implementation and uses cases in detail in this chapter. Follow along to know a lot about the recommendation systems.

What are the recommendation algorithms?

In today's era of big data, where data is exploding and people are suffering from information overload, the advent of the Recommendation System (RS) has made it a lot easier for users and bring a lot of practical value to the enterprise.

We will introduce the Collaborative Filtering (CF) algorithm is considered to be one of the most learned and researched algorithms of the recommended system in the present world. We will also introduce several other algorithms that deal with different strategies, such as based on the number of users and aligning with them and also based on no.of items that are present in them. We will introduce graph-based algorithms where unlike traditional methods discussed before can be represented not only by a matrix but also by a bipartite graph You can use a graph-based recommendation algorithm.

1) Collaborative filtering algorithm

It is a known fact that when compared to past years quantity and quality in detail we can come to a conclusion that network is increasing rapidly, which makes the problem of information overload become more and more serious. When the users have no definite information demand, they cannot get the information they are interested in from a large amount of information the rapid increase in the amount of information has also led to a large amount of information buried, unable to reach some potential users. The advent of Recommendation System (RS) is called the bridge between users and information. This is considered to be superior because it will help people get the information what they are interested to have, on the other hand, it can pass the valuable information to the potential users.

Collaborative Filtering (CF) algorithm is the most basic recommendation algorithm, this will categorically store every small thing the user has done on the website or app of their interests and recommends the items to the user. According to a different mining method s, collaborative filtering algorithms can be divided based on a number of users present and the number of items they want to link the data with. We will discuss them in detail in the next chapter.

A brief view of recommended system neural networks:
In the age of information overload, information has shown explosive growth, for example, a large number of micro-blogs are created and forwarded every day. The explosive growth of information has brought new

information to users continuously It also makes it harder for users to sift through information when they have specific needs, such as the need to find "collaborative filtering algorithms, " which can be used by social networking websites and other search engines to give access to the users based on their wishes and recommendations.

However, users do not always have a clear need. For example, on Weibo, users just want to pass the time by checking every tweet on their home page. At this time, users do not have a clear purpose In order to be able to help users filter out a batch of information they may be interested in, it is necessary to analyze the user's interest, select from the mass of information that is present in the multinational companies to develop a clear cut model integration to the recommendation system and is proposed in this background, Recommendation algorithm according to the user's preferences, and recommend to the user the goods or information corresponding to their preferences. The task of recommender systems is to connect information with users, help users find the information they are interested in, and allow some valuable information to reach potential users.

Overview of a collaborative filtering algorithm:

This famous and very well known filtering algorithm among others finds a specific pattern in the user's behavior and produces effective recommendations for the user through that pattern. It relies on data about the user's behavior in the system, for example, by reading books that the user has read, and by producing reviews of those books, which are then used to infer the user's reading preferences.

The core idea of this algorithm that takes a lot of inspiration from its predecessors is to discover user preferences by mining user history behavior data, group users based on different preferences and recommend similar items. In calculating the recommended results, it does not depend on any additional information on the items or any additional information of the user, but only on the user's rating of the item.

Measures of similarity in neural networks:

There are many methods to measure similarity, and different methods have different application fields. Similarity measurement has been used in different machine learning algorithms, such as K-Means clustering algorithm.

A) User-based collaborative filtering

This is one of the important collaborative algorithms discovered because it constantly updates with itself based on the interest of the core user. A user-based special algorithm uses different methods to understand what would happen if similar items are recommended.

Among them, the user marks the value of goods greater than or equal to 0, equal to 0 means that the user did not score the goods. This can be used to calculate different complex and unnecessary functions in the user-product Matrix and get the desired result of a matrix that can be used in further developments.

We will implement this is TensorFlow as shown below.

Python code:

```python
def userbased(caw,w,data)
input : data(mat)
#we have given input
output predict(list)
# This will give a predictable system
m,n = np.shape(data)
# 1st function
not_inter = []
for i in.append
else
exit
# 2nd function
for x in not_inter
predict[x]-w
return sorted
```

B) Item-based collaborative filtering

This is one of the natural and perfect algorithms that have been developed without any second thought and it includes: 1 importing data; 2 making a recommendation by using a certain algorithmic step based on basic characteristic components like user and items.

Now, we use the above function to implement an algorithm that can solve the complexity of structured items present. First, to enable Python to support Chinese annotations and Matrix operations, we need to add the following at the beginning of the ``item " file:

from userbase-recommend

A user-based collaborative filtering algorithm is definitely the most important and essential algorithm that needs to be learned for greater results . The basic steps include: 1 using the function load to import user merchandise data, as shown in Listing 1, and converting it into a merchandise user matrix As shown in 2 of the Program Code; 2 use similarity function to calculate similarity between products, as shown in 3 of the Program Code; 3 use function item to recommend user, as shown in 4 of the Program Code; 4 recommend top products for user based on the final score, as shown in 5 in the Program Code.

Code:

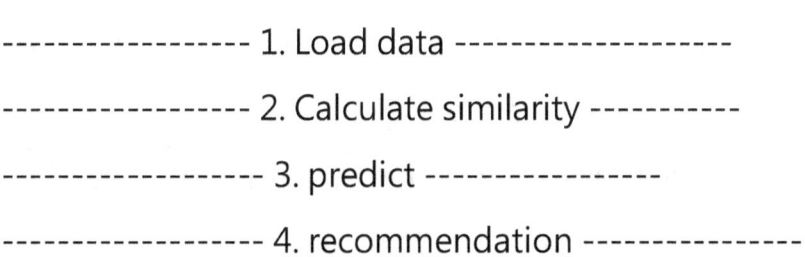

The recommended results for User 0 users using the user-based collaborative filtering algorithm is:

[(2, 5.3798287),(6,8.932342)]

2) Graph-based recommendation algorithm

In this particular well peer-reviewed algorithm user-merchandise data can be transformed into the storage form of user-merchandise Matrix, and this is perfect with all other algorithms in the first two sections or the method based on the use case of matrix importance can be used to realize the function of recommendation. At the same time the data that coexist as good one can be transformed into the storage form of the bipartite graph, in which the two subsets, V1 and V2, are respectively the set of nodes that are essential for the calculation and interpretation of the problem.

The rank algorithm which uses graphs uses nodes to define its results. By using the Personal Rank Algorithm, we can calculate the importance of all the other nodes relative to the user node, and realize the recommendation for the user.

a) Bipartite graph

Bipartite graphs are often used in many practical problems. A bipartite graph is a kind of undirected graph if in an undirected graph F vertex are defined by V and then edges are easily distinguished using the symbol e in an undirected graph. In an undirected graph V these vertices can be used to be defined with several easy descriptions like e and V.

An undirected graph G is called a Bipartite Graph, and V1 and V2 are called complementary Vertex subsets. In particular, if each vertex in V1 is adjacent to all vertices in V2, then G is called a graph that is complete and necessary for this system.

In a recommender system, the ultimate goal is to recommend the relevant item to the User Ui, at which point the item in the item list { D1, D2, ... , D5} needs to be calculated for the user Ui And generate a final list of recommendations based on importance. The PageRank algorithm is used to process the importance of ranking on the graph.

In the next section, we will discuss the PageRank algorithm. Websites like Google, Bing use PageRank algorithms to rank webpages. They are very secretive and use tons of neural network layers and complex coding to determine the number of backlinks that determine the authoritative score of that particular webpage. We will discuss in detail about it.

Page rank algorithm

The PageRank Algorithm, or PageRank, was developed by Petch and Sergey Brin in 1997. PageRank is a method to identify the rank and importance of a web page. It is important to decide the authenticity of a web page in the network that is largest that is the Internet. This also helps to determine the quality and the importance of webpages in Google's search engine. Before the PageRank algorithm was put forward, it was proposed to use the number of links in a web page for link analysis But the PageRank algorithm not only considers the number of links but also refers to the quality of web pages. By combining the number of links and the quality of web pages, the PageRank Algorithm makes the evaluation of the importance of web pages more accurate.

In search engines, some web pages have come up with many ways to cheat in order to get ahead in the rankings, a practice known as Link Spam. In a nutshell, for the above page-level Algorithm, which only considers the number of links in a page, someone has made a lot of pages to make their page (called page a) point to page A So the number of pages a link will become a lot, naturally, a page a will become very high level of the page, but such a high level of the page a is only the result of the owner of cheating, does not equal to the quality of the page is very good.

The PageRank algorithm avoids this situation because the PageRank value takes into account both the number of links and the quality of the web page, as previously stated, whereas the quality of the web page that points to page a by itself is low The result of this synthesis is that page a's page quality will not become very high, so the PageRank Algorithm on the page quality evaluation played a very good effect. The Link Analysis of a Web page can be abstracted into a graphical model.

Algorithm of Page rank

The PageRank calculation for a web page is based on two assumptions:

a) Quantitative assumptions

In the Web graph model, the more links a page node receives from other pages, the more important the page is. That is the more links to page the more important page a is.

b) Mass Assumption

The quality that links possess may be manipulated to small no authority web pages and high-quality pages pass more weight through links to other pages, so the this needs to be improved to prepare a good well-enriched algorithm that defines the conditions in detail. That is, the more important the original page that links to page the more important page a will be.

The number hypothesis is simply that on the Internet, the more links a page receives from other pages, the more important the page is. This needs to be clearly understood that there is nothing to be made up and the higher the quality of a page, the more important that page is. The algorithm that can be defined and made to be used combines these two assumptions well, making it more accurate to evaluate the importance of a web page.

Personal Rank Algorithm:

In the PageRank Algorithm, the calculated PR value is the importance degree of each node relative to the whole world, while in the recommendation problem, we want to solve the importance degree of all commodity nodes relative to a user node in the user-commodity bipartite graph shown, when a recommendation is made for user U1, it is the importance of all commodity nodes DJ relative to user U1 that needs to be calculated, not the global importance of each node.

The Personal Rank algorithm is a variant of the PageRank algorithm, which is used to calculate the importance of all commodity nodes D J relative to a user node U. If the user is U1, then the node U1 starts to move in the user-commodity bipartite graph. When it moves to any node, as the PageRank algorithm, it will choose to stop or continue to move according to a certain probability. Assuming the option to continue to walk, the current node as a new starting point, repeat the above process, until each node access probability is no longer changed.

Implementation in the Python:

With the above knowledge, we now implement the Personal Rank algorithm recommendation process, first of all, in order to be able to use the correlation function of the Matrix, at the same time, in order to make Python can support annotations, therefore, in the "personal" file to add.

Code:

```
def load(filepath) :
f = open(file)
data = []
for line r.readlines
tmp = []
f.close
return null
```

Function for pagerank:

```
items_dict = {}
# 1st rule
items k
for rule data_dict{user,keys}
# 2nd rule
for k in rank.keys()
items_dict[k] = rank[k]
#3rd rule
result sorted(items_dict.item)
return result
```

The recommend function ranks items that the user has not interacted with, based on a score calculated by the Personal Rank algorithm. In the recommend function, there are three steps: 1 find the item that the user has interacted within the user-product bipartite graph, as shown in 1 in the Program Code; 2 take all the item ratings from rank, as shown in 2 in the program code The ungraded items are sorted and returned in descending order according to the score, as shown in 3 of the Program Code.

The output of the code:

------------------Loaddata------------------

------------------ generatedict-------------

----------------personalrank----------------

iter : 0

iter : 1

iter : 2

With this, we have completed the detailed explanation of Machine learning using scikitlearn and TensorFlow in detail. Now make up your mind and practice with the will and hardwork to implement them in your machine learning applications.

Conclusion

Thank you for making it through to the end of *Machine Learning in Python*, let' s hope it was informative and able to provide you with all of the tools you need to achieve your goals whatever they may be.

The next step is to use this knowledge to develop real world machine learning applications. You can expand your knowledge by trying to learn about statistical machine learning and data analysis where you will encounter a lot of more valuable information that can be used to increase experience in the field.

Machine learning and algorithms are used in almost every software application and mobile applications nowadays. As a developer who will use these algorithmic principles in your software, you need to further improve your expertise by reading different advanced books dealing with the subject. Great books end in a great manner so does ours.

Machine learning is a very important technology in the coming days due to its wide range of availability that can help them attain and used for various applications. For example, Google translates and other software like Bing translate uses machine translation to get the desired results.

Always try to practice the skills you have mastered in virtual environments. the Internet is full of opportunities and the concepts mastered here can easily be implemented. Always use Google and stack overflow if you are stuck with any doubts.

Finally, if you found this book useful in any way, a review on Amazon is always appreciated!